Choosing
the
Miracle

Choosing

the

Miracle

Pauline Edward

Desert Lily Publications
Montreal, Canada

Cover design: Nancy Overbury
Illustrations: Alexander Marchand and Pauline Edward
V1.01

Library and Archives Canada Cataloguing in Publication

Edward, Pauline, 1954-
  Choosing the miracle / Pauline Edward.

  Includes bibliographical references.
  Issued also in electronic format.
  ISBN 978-0-9868909-0-1

  1. Course in Miracles. 2. Spiritual life. I. Title.

BP605.C68E36 2012   299'.93   C2011-907723-X

CONTENTS

FOREWORD

*P*AULINE EDWARD FIRST CONTACTED me in 2010 to see if I'd be interested in reviewing her then soon-to-be published book, *Leaving the Desert: Embracing the Simplicity of A COURSE IN MIRACLES*. She had found me through my Course website/blog: www.foraysinforgiveness.com, and felt the spark of recognition of a kindred Course journeyer and fellow student of the brilliant ACIM scholar and teacher, Ken Wapnick. Her intuition, as usual; was spot on. We became fast friends and fellow fans. She has been instrumental in helping me on a worldly level, but also, and most importantly, in providing the kind of gentle listening and support for my forgiveness practice that helps me remember the only real relationship we are truly cultivating here if we have chosen to awaken from a dream of separation: our relationship with the part of our mind that never fell asleep. The part of our mind that knows our only real relationship remains the one in which we continue to thrive united, eternally loving and seamlessly fused in peace with our creator.

Pauline—whose many talents include a fearless ability to embrace technology that I would prefer to ignore—soon had me signed up on Skype. We began regularly conversing, sharing our writing and teaching troubles and triumphs but mainly our mind-healing process; insights gleaned from harnessing the transformative power of forgiveness ACIM-style in the classroom of our daily lives. Learning to honestly observe our attraction to the special interests, preferences, judgments, opinions, and blaming impulses of our mind on ego and choose instead for the inner teacher of oneness. Learning to rely on the memory of our true wholeness in our one mind always available to dissolve our belief in the ego's shenanigans in return for every sincere call for its gentle vision and winning smile. Although quite different in our approach to the world and the Course at the personality level, I recognize (and rejoice) in Pauline as a fellow journeyer as committed to finding her way home—at times, come hell or high water—as I am, and equally willing to catch wrong-minded thinking, resign again as her own teacher, and ask for a better way.

In her previous book, *Leaving the Desert*, Pauline recounted her struggle to wrap her head around the confounding (to the ego, the part of our mind that believes we pulled off the "tiny, mad, idea" of separation from our source and now exist as individuals vying for survival in an imaginary universe of fragmented form) metaphysical position presented in *A Course in Miracles*. The startling and consistent revelation that the world in which we believe we interact as bodies does not in truth exist. The blasphemous—to organized religions revolving around a dualistic God made in the ego's unstable image—idea that God did not create this world and in fact knows nothing of it. By delving deeply into the text, workbook, and related materials Pauline honestly shared her growing understanding of the Course's unique, mind-healing, forgiveness practice that teaches us to take responsibility for the seeming external problems in our relationships back to the source in the one mind and ask for a different interpretation from the part of our mind that can truly see, smile, and share its perception of uninterrupted wholeness. Along the way, she began to confront her own fear of relinquishing the special identity we all use to push that authentic, all-inclusive and enduring Love away.

In *Choosing the Miracle*, Pauline offers an even more intimate glimpse of the forgiveness of what never was and the dawning realization that only God is; she is closer than she thought; truly awake in perfect, eternal Love, simply dreaming of exile. She recounts the many ways the ego tries to join our journey from mindlessness to mindfulness citing concrete, heartfelt examples from her own life. She explains the crucial process of looking at the wrong mind (ego) with our right mind (Holy Spirit/Jesus/that symbol of the part of our mind that remembered to laugh at the guilty thought of fragmenting infinite wholeness) to illuminate the concealed purpose of proving we exist but it's not our fault. And she reminds us we are never forgiving something real; merely our misperceptions.

Pauline deftly cautions against looking to form for evidence of our progress or lack of it with this Course when in truth, ACIM is always taking us in the other direction (back to the decision-making mind). She shares her increasingly intimate dialogue with Jesus and growing guidance and faith in the true possibility of awakening juxtaposed with a heightened awareness of the ego's increasingly sneaky ways. She also expresses a growing, experiential certainty that everyone here (including the false self we identify with) suffers from the same delusion of a split mind and therefore deserves a loving, compassionate response informed by the inner teacher of loving compassion.

This book brims with practical advice for the earnest homeward traveler illuminated by real life examples of how to stop ourselves and choose again for inner peace whenever something "out there" seems all too real and our resistance to changing our mind threatens to overwhelm us. It is a beautiful, must-have handbook for any Course student seriously committed to learning to smile at the folly of separate interests and know that—at any and every seeming moment no matter what seems to arise in our dream—we can choose peace.

Susan Dugan
Author of *Extraordinary Ordinary Forgiveness*

AUTHOR'S NOTE AND ACKNOWLEDGMENTS

*T*HIS BOOK WAS NEARLY three quarters of the way finished when I hit a wall. Although it appeared as a very high wall that would take a very long time and a whole lot of effort to be climbed, as it turned out, it simply needed to be risen above and left behind. This passing hurdle resulted in a shift in perception that left me reeling, and by the same token, wondering what to do with, among most aspects of my life, my writing. I simply could not complete, let alone publish this book. Besides which, there was nothing left to be said. I had found peace, and I knew where and how to look for the presence of God. Left to my own devices, I would simply have allowed myself to settle in this most wonderful of states, content with the simple knowledge that God is, right here, right now. I had desire for nothing more than this. I could get a job in a flower shop, and spend the remaining years of my life in peaceful simplicity.

I could have done just that, but I had sufficient wisdom to understand that the purpose of my life would remain unfulfilled should I resign myself thus, and my purpose had always been to work with people, and to write. Still, that did not clarify what I should do with the chapters I had written, material which no longer fit my new perspective. I considered scrapping the entire manuscript and starting something new, perhaps at a later date. For over two months, time I had specifically set aside for the completion of this work, I put it on hold and simply let the dust of my new understanding settle. When the time was right, I would be guided as to what to do.

And I was. Early one autumn morning, I awoke with very clear guidance. Other than normal editing, I was to leave the sections I had written intact. I would then proceed to describe the experiences that had led to the shift in perception, and complete the book as originally outlined, well, more or less. I think my dear guide was being gentle with me, for this revision ended up being a lot of work! But, no matter. This book has a purpose, and I am honoured to have had a role to play in bringing a sliver of light to my brothers and sisters, even though it caused me to experience more than a few moments of great fear and uncertainty.

It is with the deepest gratitude and love that I offer this work to the members of our small *Course in Miracles* study group. Together, we have grown much over the years. A special thanks to poet Michael J. Miller for proofreading the manuscript, and for sharing his poetry.

This work has reached completion in large part because of feedback from clients and readers. It is in the sharing of their experiences, questions and doubts, the expression of their desire and thirst for the truth and their longing for peace and wholeness that my own journey has been fuelled.

A very special thank you to Alexander Marchand, author of *The Universe Is a Dream*, for graciously providing the cool illustrations for this book (except for the invitation from the ego found in Chapter 10, a wanton lapse into creative self-expression on the part of yours truly ☺), and to my dear friend, Susan Dugan, who, in my moment of darkness, wisely reminded me that the ego lies, and it lies and it lies!

I will remain forever grateful to Mr. Homer Lin, facilitator of the Banqiao ACIM Study Group in Taiwan who followed the inspiration that allowed our paths to cross at a most critical moment of my journey. When allowed, miracles will occur in the form most needed and thus, most appropriate for all of God's Children. Thank you my dear friend.

Time to rise

by Michael J. Miller

It seems like all hope is lost;
Died, God dead and nothing remains but despair;
An empty shell of a life.

Facing the emptiness, the end,
with the last breath comes a whisper…
a vision… of another world…

The Father calls, seems distant at first,
but the feeling begins to grow;
an increasing willingness,
to yield to the Father's grace.

Do you know Christ passes no one by?
Do you know He loves you?

There is the Word of God. He has spoken.
And all false tongues shall cease to speak:
this is your awakening.

Renounce your false self and give way to the Father.
This ego is not You. Yield to Higher Self.

I cease to speak. I am quiet.
And from this stillness I reach out
beyond myself to Greater Wisdom.
Not mine, but Thy Will be done.

It will enchant you,
It will delight you,
It will transform you,

Bringing the darkness to the light.

It is time to rise,
rise from your seeming death,
and awaken unto Him!

What will the death of death look like?
Just to be curious.
Wondering what new colours will arise;
what will come into view?
Aren't you just a little curious?

What will I see, and what will I be,
when all blocks to the awareness of Love's Presence
are let go?
When all pain and fear and hell are gone,
what will I awaken to?

It is a gradual process.
Gently taken by the hand,
we are led up a staircase leading to Heaven,
each step bringing us closer,
each small flittering of our eyelids,
another glimpse of the glory beyond.

Why dilly-dally with hell
when Heaven's right around the corner!

Heaven is now—within your reach now!

Can you still justify condemning yourself,
or another part of you as a brother,
when you could be free?

A holy instant away from bliss, peace.
I am insane to throw away Heaven for hell!

Begin to awaken.
Be still.
And know that He is God.
There is nothing to fear…

REFERENCES

References to *A Course in Miracles* (ACIM) correspond to the numbering system of the Text (T), Workbook (W), Manual for Teachers (M) and Clarification of Terms (C) used in the Third Edition. For example:

T-27.VIII.6:2–5 corresponds to Text, Chapter 27, Section VIII, Paragraph 6, Sentences 2 to 5.

W-pI.132.5:1–3 corresponds to Workbook, Part I, Lesson 132, Paragraph 5, Sentences 1 to 3.

M-16.4:6 corresponds to Manual for Teachers, Question 16, Paragraph 4, Sentence 6.

C-3.4:1 corresponds to Clarification of Terms, Term 3, Paragraph 4, Sentence 1.

Introduction

We go to Heaven, and the path is straight. Only if we attempt to wander can there be delay, and needless wasted time on thorny byways. God alone is sure, and He will guide our footsteps. He will not desert His Son in need, nor let him stray forever from his home. (W-pI.200.9:2–5)

*A*S MUCH AS I have always enjoyed writing, I must admit that *Leaving the Desert* was the most difficult book for me to complete. In fact, my resistance to exploring the radical and uncompromising message of *A Course in Miracles* was so acute that there were numerous times when I honestly thought I would never see it to publication. It simply took too much out of me. Resistance notwithstanding, given my trademark tenacious temperament I persisted and eventually, much to my relief, saw it through to its rightful finish. Though I had become aware of the fact that writing would be an integral part of my learning and healing process, this had to be the most challenging bit of learning and healing I had ever encountered. In a way, it was a spiritual rite of passage of sorts, a required challenge, necessary for preparing the way for the remainder of the journey home.

After having written the chapter on specialness, a favourite of readers, as it turned out, I had the very strong, indisputably clear impulse to stop writing. At the very least, I needed to put some distance between myself and the object of my literary expression. In my haste to wrap it up and get as far away from the subject as possible, several sections were cut from the outline. Enough had been said, I thought, as I completed the final revision. People interested in learning about *A Course in Miracles* would have to get what they needed by reading the big blue book for themselves.

Relieved of the dark task, I handed the manuscript to my editor, sent out review copies and placed the whole matter in the hands of the Holy Spirit. I boldly declared that I would never again write another book, certainly not a book that stirred the cauldron of deep-seated sin, guilt and fear. When Course student and poet Michael Miller, who was at the time proof-reading the manuscript, suggested that I had set up the book for a follow-up, I replied, "Write your own goddamn book!" Having experienced more than my fair share of pain in the arms, back, neck and shoulders, not to mention the horrors of having delved into the dark corners of my unconscious mind during the eighteen months I spent working on it, I wasn't interested in writing another word, let alone another book. No more!

When I look back and wonder how it was that I made it through that very intense year (a number 7 Personal Year in the 9-year numerology cycle), I see that things happened simply as they were meant to happen. From where I stood, there really had been no alternatives. I had followed the pathway of my life's voyage just as it had been mapped out, right on through to its rightful destination. Nevertheless, this last stretch of the journey had left me feeling as though the carpet of my life had been pulled right out from under me and I wasn't quite sure yet how, or even if I would again land on level ground.

For the first time ever, I had no clear goals ahead of me, no unfulfilled yearnings, no action plan, no to-do list, nor any driving need for accomplishment. Other than attending to the basic necessities of life, of which there seemed to be an incessantly growing number in a world that had sustained a massive technological invasion, I had no significant worldly ambitions. Most long-held desires and beliefs had vanished and I felt as though I was nowhere, in an existential no-man's land with no specific destination and only fleeting reminders of what lay on the abandoned avenues of the past.

I had come too far in my study and understanding of the message of *A Course in Miracles* to turn back, yet, though my old beliefs clearly had lost their meaning and no longer served a purpose, my tender new learning had yet to set firm roots in what would flourish into the next season of my life. The canvas of my journey had been repainted; I awaited the light that would show me the way.

In the quiet of the weeks that followed the completion of my manuscript, I simply allowed everything I had learned and experienced in the previous months to settle into my being. More and more I sought solitude, silence and quiet. My new motto was: The simpler, the better. A warm feeling of peaceful surrender enveloped me as I realized that the message of *A Course in Miracles* was in fact very simple and practical, but more than that, it was a teaching I could incorporate into my life no matter the circumstances. It was a spirituality I could work with—a practical, down-to-earth person such as myself—which was a miracle in itself. Little by little, as I observed my responses to everyday situations, my dark companions—the most illustrious among them being fear, guilt, anger, impatience and specialness—began to lose their hold on me. With growing certainty, I knew that I now walked with mighty companions by my side. Faith came into full bloom as the shadows of doubt and uncertainty that had for too long hovered at the edges of my awareness dissipated. Instead, I welcomed each opportunity to look at, and release, the darkness that remained, for each spot of darkness forgiven revealed more of the light beyond.

I toggled between states of deep peace, at times accompanied by tears of profound relief, and the joy of having found such an incredible spiritual path. While out on my daily walks, listening to Ken Wapnick workshops on my MP3 player, I smiled. I even smiled at dogs; poor slobbering fools sauntering along at the end of their leashes. It even briefly crossed my mind that perhaps, when my cat Maggie passed away, I might consider a canine companion. Serious and reserved by nature, I didn't do *smile*; at least not at strangers, and especially not at dogs. But there I'd be, walking down the street, listening to my favourite teacher expound on sin, guilt and fear, and I would be smiling, and frequently, even laughing. I'm sure the neighbours must have thought I had lost it, and in a way, I suppose I had. I had lost the need to take this world so seriously. What a tremendous relief to lose such an insufferable burden.

Arf.

The self I had spent over half a century cultivating, nurturing and grooming was growing increasingly insignificant. The voice of the focused, serious, intense, dedicated, persistent self that had stood boldly behind all my past decisions and actions grew fainter. The long, dark, winding leg of the journey—the incessant search for the truth—had ended and was now veering in a new, brighter direction. But I was unsure as to what to do, or how to approach this new direction, and oftentimes, I was not quite sure of who I was or who I was meant to be any more. Now what? I thought. I had all this understanding, all this knowledge, and the willingness to practise this powerful new spirituality whenever an opportunity arose, but, then what?

I needed to understand the nature of the next step on this strange new terrain, but who could answer my questions about feelings I could barely articulate? Through business networking and consultations, I had met thousands of people over the years, yet there was no one to whom I could ask my burning questions. *Then what?* I needed to know more about this spiritual process, about its consequences. There was, I concluded, only one person in the world who could help me. After exchanging a couple of telephone messages, we finally connected. Patiently and most graciously, Ken Wapnick answered all my questions, including the one that troubled me the most.

"Then what," I asked, eager to better understand what a life dedicated to the practice of forgiveness in pursuit of the only goal that mattered—awakening from the dream—would mean while everything in the world seemed to have lost all meaning.

"Then it's no longer you," he replied with utmost simplicity.

Huh! Then it's no longer me. It was simple.

That was all I needed to know. I mulled over those words for months, contemplating the thought of being free of the "self" with which I still identified. Mocking jeers from my unwilling companion—the ego—would occasionally surface as spiteful reminders that I was not yet quite ready to give it up—*Right, then it's no longer you!* But there was no rush; it could—and would—be a gentle, peaceful process. I would be patient with myself. In time, I would be ready to let this self go simply to be replaced by a far greater Self. In time, it would no longer be *me*, and the more I thought about it, the more it sounded like a good thing. In truth, since time is also part of the illusion and never really *was*, the "self" to which I clung never really was either. Which meant that in truth, what remained was the Self which is a reflection of the Oneness of God, the Self which includes all "Selves," the Self in which you and I are joined as one. Though it seemed like a most unrealistic goal, this became the experience I sought; a new destination was written onto the road map of my life.

Finding Normal

I think I could very easily have allowed myself to sink deeper and engage more completely in my newfound state of spiritual grace, but I knew that I would at some point have to get back to the real world or, perhaps more accurately, the dream world. There were bills to be paid, which the utilities companies certainly would not perceive as illusory, so I needed to return my attention to my consulting practice. All those months spent writing had depleted what little funds I had and I could no longer afford to sit in blissful contemplation. I busied myself with the publication of *Leaving the Desert* and returned to my normal life, at least, what was normal for me: an astrologer politely networking with real estate agents, business coaches and investment advisors, secretly aware that all of it is little more than the result of a tiny, mad idea. Be normal, Ken Wapnick reminds repeatedly. So, in an attempt to be normal, I renewed my

Chamber of Commerce membership, signed up for networking luncheons and cocktails and started a session of group coaching for writers.

Still, even as life returned to a semblance of normalcy, I continued to feel somewhat disconnected. There was no hurry. In fact, I seemed to have adopted a rather detached attitude about pretty much everything I did, which was not normal for the driven, hard-working individual that once inhabited this body. Other than paying the bills, there was little motivation for doing anything that belonged to this world. While the world seemed to be speeding up around me, I shifted the pace of my activities down to a very slow second gear, just fast enough to keep up with matters at hand. I simplified as many aspects of my business and daily activities as possible and took things one day at a time. Still, the more I focused on the mundane affairs of life, the more I wanted to pull away. I began to imagine one day abandoning my astrology practice, even if it meant getting a part-time job somewhere, a favourite place in my imaginings being a flower shop. "I want to go live in a tree," I would say. When a flower shop opened up in walking distance from my home, I took this as a sign; if I needed to, I could always apply for a job. It was a relief to know I had a viable option.

It wasn't that I no longer wanted to work with clients; it was more that I no longer knew how to work with the tools of my trade. Or, perhaps it was that I did not know quite how to work with people who believed that their lives were *caused* by external forces such as planetary transits and numbers. From my new perspective, I understood that the circumstances of our lives are a reflection of our decision for separation. They are not caused by anything outside our minds. In fact, the entire cosmos and any symbolism we might derive from it is a projection of that one thought of separation; all of our experiences are the result of our ongoing decision to maintain this belief.

There were times when I felt unable to help my clients because I could not support their beliefs that their pain and unhappiness came from some outside source such as a cruel and insensitive spouse, a miserable, unsatisfactory job, or a broken-down body. I sensed their pain, their fears and their sorrows, saw the darkness of their confusion and recognized that their grief came from a deeply buried belief in separation. Many of these people believed that if you were a good person, then good things should happen to you. If many people became good persons, then the world would become the good place it was meant to be. How could I tell them that in the darkest recesses of their minds, they actually believed they were the home of evil, darkness and sin and the world was an outward picture of that belief and therefore could never be a place of peace?

For several months, I felt pulled between the dual poles of my existence: my work with the Course, on which I could not count to pay the bills, and my work as an astrologer, which paid the bills, but where, with my clients, I could no longer be entirely forthcoming. My situation was a reflection of the inherent duality of one who, on the one hand, identified with the separated self in a body in the world and, on the other hand, had started to remember that there is another part of the mind that knows that only a state of perfect oneness and wholeness can possibly be true.

The Course tells us that there is no hierarchy of illusions, that there is no order of difficulty in miracles, and that we should make it all the same. I knew very well that if I quit my practice and went to work in a flower shop, I would encounter just as many difficulties, though perhaps in different forms. So I practised looking at my brothers without judgment and learned to handle their questions with kindness, compassion and understanding, and in particular, respect for where they were on their individual journeys. I became adept at deflecting questions that concerned the cause of situations and circumstances and focused on listening to where they were at so as to be as helpful as possible. Sometimes, all they needed was the reassurance that help could always be found when one was ready to receive it. My increased openness and compassion was rewarded with deeper insights and greater helpfulness, and I found more meaning in my work.

Interestingly, and perhaps not surprisingly, my practice began to shift as readers of *Making Peace with God* and *Leaving the Desert* requested consultations from the perspective of the Course. This gave me the opportunity to inject a much-needed breath of fresh air into my approach, making consultation work more rewarding. I suppose I should not have been surprised by this, but most were struggling with the practical application of the Course's teaching in their lives. Particularly confusing for all Course students I encountered was the idea that the world is an illusion, something with which I too struggled. Who were these seemingly separated selves having experiences that were, to them, so very real?

Nudged Back into Writing

Not long after my declaration of independence from writing, having replaced writing time with household tasks such as laundry, cleaning the house, mowing the lawn or running errands—all of which I found to be pleasantly monastic in their goalless simplicity—it occurred to me that I felt lost without a book-in-the-making. Barely a couple of weeks had passed after having handed the manuscript of *Leaving the Desert* to my editor when I awoke with the very clear thought that I was to write another book. *No way! Not another one. Can't do it. No way!* But the guidance was strong and clear. In this new book, I would pick up the themes that had been dropped from the outline of *Leaving the Desert* and further explore the practical side of how to live with *A Course in Miracles*.

Despite my sincere oath to never again write on the terrifying trio of sin, guilt and fear, I felt excited about this new book project. It appeared that it was nearly impossible to shake the life-long writing bug; it was a chronic condition. I sat at the computer, set up the book files, started an outline and then put my laptop back on the dining room table, one of my favourite writing spots. Though

Choosing the Miracle had been conceived, I did not start work on it right away, as I was still unconvinced that more needed to be said. It would gestate for a while, and that was okay. It just felt good to know that there was a project on the back burner for whenever the urge to write arose. There was something in the world for me to *do*. As an avid *doer*, this meant that life was really returning to normal.

Though not actively working on the book, I sketched out personal reflections and experiences in a journal and took note of questions asked by clients and Course students. Interestingly, quite often these questions were related to the very topics I had dropped from *Leaving the Desert* or subjects I had sketched out in my journal. Nearly every time, these queries came when I had been questioning the need to write another book. As the weeks turned into months, I continued to toggle between my desire to write, and the sense that nothing more needed to be written. Again, here was a reflection of the dualistic nature of my split mind: to write, or not to write; to be heard, or to be silent. The inner battle of truth versus illusion sought expression in the world outside, making itself heard.

Just before the start of the new year, I had a visit from channeller Lisa LaJoie. Since that first reading recounted in the Introduction of *Leaving the Desert*, we had become good friends. Once again, though I had not actively sought out a channelled reading, it appeared that this was one of the ways in which I would receive the guidance I needed from my teacher, Jesus. In this reading it was pointed out that on my journey I was called to share my experiences. "Your nature is built to share, even if you are a hermit."

An interesting image Lisa received was that of Buddha and Jesus sitting in a tree with roots above the ground. "You are a tree, with its branches and roots above the ground, free to move ahead," she told me. "Choice exists only in separation. You are going to live without choice; on the tree, there is no more choice. Choose not to choose; seek only knowingness. In knowingness, you act differently, though you can have your own thoughts." This imagery was all the more interesting given my curious recurring quip about wanting to live in a tree!

Despite my preference for maintaining a low profile, I was told to be fearless in sharing my experience of, as well as my love for Jesus, as I proceed on my journey. "Share thoughts of knowing who we are in truth. You are going somewhere new. Stop standing down. Living the Course exists for you, J exists," Lisa added with emphasis. "Humanity is confused; be unafraid to express your life. You are not an observer anymore. You have a place to stand. It starts inside. The Course got you to the point where you could ask questions and choose. In your book, ask questions. Share more in the questions." Again, this was a request which I found interesting since I had already begun to take notes in the form of questions to be explored. "Share his love in the community; comfort and strength come by accepting him." I would have the comfort and the strength I needed, Jesus reassured me, since I had accepted to take this journey with him.

"Stop talking about going home. Know that you are home. This is the miracle." Although I liked the sound of those words, I believed I had a very long way to go before I was anywhere near home, and so I was not about to stop my quest any time soon. Besides, knowing that I was home was much easier said than done, at least from my limited ego-invested perspective.

Though I had always been somewhat skeptical of channelled material, I had little doubt that Lisa was channelling Jesus. The experience of the love we shared together in his presence was clearly not of this world. However, during this reading, I wondered if some of his message might have gotten garbled in the transmission. Lisa was not a Course student and so, when she said that life was about "Finding the grace in our choice to come here" and that my life was about "healing of the grief over being born human; the miracle of the soul coming into the body; the acceptance of having both worlds inside, the soul and the body," I chalked it up to her inexperience with the metaphysics of the Course. The body is part of the world, and is therefore part of the illusion. I certainly could not celebrate the miracle of the soul coming into the body!

Another part of that session left me feeling somewhat uncomfortable. "There is more to the Course to be revealed, about the journey, about coming here. I'll be back when it's time. Do people understand that God is here? That I am here? In this density? The way you think about the Course brings separation. There is more to that book. It's about choice. Then, there is living in knowing."

It was true that I held the Course in very high regard; and yes, perhaps I had made it a bit special, okay, *very* special. But that there was *more* to the Course? That God or Jesus were *here*, in the illusion? These points did not make sense to me. Much had been said about living in the world, in a body, while all I wanted was to awaken from the dream, leave the body and leave the world. Where I would go after departing the body and the world remained a mystery. Though I didn't fully understand the message, I left it at that, trusting that, in time, understanding would come.

If Lisa's reading wasn't enough of a nudge toward writing, there were encouraging emails from readers. One woman even expressed sadness at the thought of reaching the end of *Leaving the Desert*, reading very slowly, not eager to be without anything to read. Most stated that they looked forward to my next book. Readers indicated that the personal style of the writing was not only appreciated, but also very helpful. Despite that we all came from vastly different backgrounds from around the globe, they related to my experiences, shared in the sorrows, the pains and the joys, the search for wholeness, and sensed the hope.

So, once again, I began to give serious thought to writing, pondering this introductory section in particular, wondering what was the best way to write it, which point of view to take, whether or not I should continue to write in the first person, or if I should adopt a more impersonal, third person point of view. Increasingly, I had begun to feel little need to make my presence felt in my writing. The author of my books, the figure in my dream, was losing its foothold in my mind as the dreamer of the dream was learning to look from an entirely different vantage point, choosing a way of looking that was more whole, more peaceful, a development with which I was very pleased.

I searched my bookshelves for ideas on writing style and point of view, noting that Thomas Merton had continued to write in the first person long after the publication of *The Seven Storey Mountain*. This debate, which went on for several weeks was, once again, a reflection of the battle of my split mind: to write in the first person or the third person; to be visible, or to make myself invisible. Finally, I decided to write in the same voice and style as my previous books. This is what I knew; this is what my readers wanted; this is what I had been guided to do; and in the end, this was the simplest solution.

Stop standing down... Be fearless in sharing your experience.

Once that hurdle was overcome, another took its place. Never at a loss to find objects of projection, the inner battle found a new outlet. In recent months, I had noticed that there was an increasing number of *Course in Miracles* books on the market, and good books too. Did the world need to be burdened with yet *another* one? Then I thought of the hundreds of hours of Ken Wapnick workshops I had listened to over and over again, and Gary Renard's book, *The Disappearance of the Universe*, which I had read eight times, and how at each listening, or each reading, my learning and understanding had grown, if only by one small step. Sometimes, it was those tiny bits of learning that were the most significant, as when I read Alexander Marchand's wonderful book, *The Universe Is a Dream*. Who would have thought it possible to gain significant insights about *A Course in Miracles* from a graphic-novel—a comic book!

I understood that varying our learning aids could be very helpful. In fact, while being taught the same thing in the same way repeatedly could be helpful for establishing a foundation of learning, this approach would eventually be used by the wrong-minded ego to devise clever objections and resistances to learning, a hard lesson I would learn first-hand. Being taught the same thing in a radical new way might be helpful in throwing the ego off guard. So, I concluded, perhaps there was room in the library of the world for another Course book after all.

Yet another battle laid to rest, I placed the matter in the hands of the Holy Spirit, trusting that inspiration would come when it was time. But days passed and again, my split mind spoke out in its defence pointing out that perhaps I was not really spiritual enough to pursue this path, much less write another book on the most significant spirituality of the century. Had Gary Renard not characterized *Leaving the Desert* as being "one of the most practical spiritual books ever written"? Who was I kidding! Maybe I was too practical!

But Jesus repeatedly tells us that the Course is very practical. It would have to be so, otherwise, how could we possibly study and practise a teaching that says that there is no world and what we see is an outside picture of an inward condition that we don't even know exists? And so it was that while getting back to normal, I realized that I am indeed a practical person and, not surprisingly, my writing is likely to reflect that fact. Again, in keeping with my newfound creed of simplicity, this is the approach I decided to adopt. I put the matter back into the hands of the Holy Spirit; at some point I would know what, when, and how to write the book, if that is what I was meant to do.

Early one spring morning, as my awareness was winding its way out from dreams of sleep to the waking dream, I heard a chime, a cheery, musical wave and then these words, in my own voice: *God, here I am!* In that instant, everything became crystal clear in my mind. I reminded myself of the workbook lesson I had read the day before, *I trust my brothers who are one with me*, got up, made my coffee, grabbed a muffin and sat down to write. Writing would continue to be a significant part of my healing process, as it required that I look deep in my mind, and the simpler and more logical my thinking process, the deeper would be my understanding. Writing kept the teaching of the Course very close, so that whatever happened in my life, I knew where to look. Since we are all of one mind, I would write with my brothers and sisters on the journey, in my customary, personal and practical style, an approach that I hoped would be most helpful for all. And so it was that I began the next leg of my journey together with you, my reader, deepening our understanding and lessening the fear that is but a small veil over the truth that lies within each of us.

My brother, you are part of God and part of me. When you have at last looked at the ego's foundation without shrinking you will also have looked upon ours. I come to you from our Father to offer you everything again. Do not refuse it in order to keep a dark cornerstone hidden, for its protection will not save you. I give you the lamp and I will go with you. You will not take this journey alone. I will lead you to your true Father, Who hath need of you, as I have. Will you not answer the call of love with joy? (T-11.in.IV.4)

Chapter 1

IN SEARCH OF TRUE HOLINESS

All that is needful is to train our minds to overlook all little senseless aims, and to remember that our goal is God. (W-pII.258.1:1)

Only the Holy

WHEN I WAS GROWING up, I believed that holiness was reserved for a very few select, saintly souls. From a Catholic perspective, holiness belonged to God's special chosen ones, most of whom were made to endure tremendous suffering and sacrifice, with a perverse emphasis placed on the *suffering*. In fact, suffering seemed to be a key component of holiness and, by my limited understanding of all things theological and a natural aversion to suffering, holiness was certainly not a state that I believed was, nor ever would be, within the range of my sinful, unblessed reach. Clearly, with a temperament that was more hedonistic than holy, I knew very well that I could never be sufficiently motivated to endure the suffering required of the saintly and therefore had literally no hope, nor reasonable expectation of ever attaining any significant degree of holiness.

Yet, not one to back down from an impossible challenge, I clung to a curious attraction for what was for me a lofty, though seemingly unattainable, state. Over the years, I did come to learn that throughout history there have been some truly inspired Catholics, as well as many beautiful souls from other religions and spiritual paths whose holiness was not entirely founded on suffering. This further piqued my curiosity and, despite what I had been taught, also kept me from completely accepting that holiness was reserved for a select, suffering, or non-suffering, few. If God were fair, then holiness must be for all; as our Creator and Father, He would love all His children equally, and all His children must be equally holy.

A couple of years into my work with *A Course in Miracles*, I was compelled to read once again some of the books that had moved my spirit during my youthful quest for the truth, works whose messages were, at the time, very far above my spiritual pay grade, yet, which shed a tiny spark of light in the shadows of my slumbering soul. In the tales of these saints and mystics—St. John of the Cross, St. Teresa of Avila, Thomas à Kempis, Ramana Maharshi—I recognized that, though the forms of our journeys may differ vastly, the yearning for an experience of closeness to God is a reflection of the memory we all share, the deeply buried remembrance of our true state of oneness in the Kingdom of Heaven. It is a calling that transcends history, education, culture or religious tradition, a yearning that is beyond words or language. It is this tiny spark of remembrance that causes us to question the reality of separation from our Father and that ignites our curiosity about the truth of who we really are, as God created us.

Venkataraman was not yet sixteen when he heard the call. Raised in the comfort of a middle-class family, he enjoyed all manner of sports and outdoor activities and also did well in school. One day he met an elderly relative who had recently returned from a trip to Arunachala, what he thought of as a mythical sacred place. In *Ramana Maharshi and the Path of Self-Knowledge*, Arthur Osborne tells the story of the young sage's call to awakening. "[T]he sudden realization that the holy hill was a real, tangible place on earth that men could visit overwhelmed Venkataraman with awe so that he could only stammer out: *What! From Arunachala? Where is that?*" Not long after that fateful encounter with his relative, the young

Venkataraman came across a copy of the Periapuranam, the life stories of the sixty-three Tamil Saints. The beauty, the faith and the divine fervour expressed by these holy persons so inspired him with awe and wonder that his outlook on life and the Divine was forever changed. "Something greater than all dreamlands, greater than all ambition, was here proclaimed real and possible, and the revelation thrilled him with blissful gratitude." He experienced "a wave of bewildering joy at perceiving that the Divine can be made manifest on earth."

Everything that had ever meant anything to the young schoolboy faded as he slipped into increasingly frequent states of a peaceful awareness that transcended mind and body. It was then only a matter of weeks before he attained a state of complete awakening, an experience which he described thus: "as I stood there waves of emotion overwhelmed me. The soul had given up its hold on the body when it renounced the 'I-am-the-body' idea and it was seeking some fresh anchorage; hence the frequent visits to the temple and the outpouring of the soul in tears." What was most interesting was that he had never before shown any particular interest in anything spiritual or religious. This was simply Venkataraman's time to awaken, a young man who came to be known as Sri Ramana Maharshi, a holy man who came to show us the way.

Though perhaps lacking in theological sophistication, or perhaps because of that fact, I was very moved by the words of Brother Lawrence, a man who knew that there is only one thought worth keeping. The true power of his holiness resided in the simplicity of his faith and his complete and uncompromising devotion to being in the presence of God. Though this is a work I discovered only in recent years—one of those books that just happens to pop into one's life at the appropriate time—it served to strengthen my resolve to seek within and find a faith that was absolute and unshakable. Unlike Brother Lawrence, I still believed in the necessity of books and methods of going to God, a belief that was soon about to change.

Having found in many books different methods of going to God, and divers practices of the spiritual life, I thought this would serve rather to puzzle me than facilitate what I sought after, which was nothing but how to become wholly God's. This made me resolve to give the all for the all; so after having given myself wholly to God… *I renounced, for the love of Him, everything that was not He; and I began to live as if there was none but He and I in the world.* (*The Practice of the Presence of God and the Spiritual Maxims*, Brother Lawrence.)

While reading works such as these in my late teens had merely shed a faint glimmer of light in a distant part of my mind, as I read them again after having been immersed in the Course decades later, the light grew to fill my entire awareness with a beauty so wholly engaging that it literally drove me to tears. The faint remembrance was becoming a recognition of a truth so overwhelming that I could no longer ignore its call. It seemed that the journey of my life had not only come full circle, it had found its true meaning and purpose.

To remain on track, all I needed was to ask myself one question: What was my first thought when I awoke this morning? Was it of God? Was it a thought of gratitude for the many opportunities the day would bring to help take me one step closer to the presence of God? Was it a thought of profound relief from the simple knowledge that the children of God need not worry or stress or be anxious about anything that belongs to a made-up world? A world that is little more than a temporary interlude between the time of our return home and a moment of curiosity about a thought of separation that could not ever be real?

The Truth Is Simple, But…

Oneness is simply the idea God is. And in His Being, He encompasses all things. No mind holds anything but Him. We say "God is," and then we cease to speak, for in that knowledge words are meaningless. (W-pI.169.5:1–4)

A Course in Miracles states the truth thus: God is. Period. A truly holy person would have no need to pursue the matter any further. What else is there to ponder? What thoughts do you hold in your mind today? How to acquire more money? Fame? Power? Influence? How to change the world? How to obtain what you want from a special love partner? How to make your body appear more attractive? How to convince someone to love you? How to prove yourself right in the face of an authoritative parent?

If only God and His creation is true, then anything in which God appears to be absent cannot be true and therefore must be a lie, an illusion, a dream, a substitute for the truth. Yet, this is not what we really think, since we believe that God is somewhere up in Heaven, and we are here, in bodies, authors of books and readers of books, in a world that makes more of a case for its reality in form than as illusion. If we truly believed that only God is true, we would know that He must be everywhere and in everything, in which case, we would not need *A Course in Miracles* or any other spirituality for that matter. In fact, we would no longer be having an experience of separation from the truth in the form of a self in a body with a so-called distinct and unique life, for experience would tell us that we are one with God. So, how is it possible to reconcile the truth with our very real evidence to the contrary?

> If you want to be like me I will help you, knowing that we are alike. If you want to be different, I will wait until you change your mind. I can teach you, but only you can choose to listen to my teaching. (T-8.IV.6:3–5)

Either Jesus is expressing the truth and everything in and of this world is a lie, or he is lying. Either he is right and we are wrong; or he is wrong and we are right. More importantly, who among us wants to admit that they are wrong, especially about every single thing they have ever held and continue to hold to be true? Unless we are willing to at least consider the possibility that Jesus is right, and we are wrong, we are not likely to get very far on this journey. We are asked to question everything we believe and, ultimately, must be prepared to choose one belief over another, illusion, or truth. Either God is true and what we see as the world is illusory, or the world is true and God is myth. It must be one or the other, but not both; and at all times, what we believe remains our choice.

Luckily, we are not expected to fully understand the implications of this extraordinary teaching, nor even to fully accept it, at least not in the early stages of our work with the Course. In fact, at first it is not unusual to feel outraged and confused at its confounding statement of the truth. We are asked only to be willing to give it some thought and above all, give it a chance to begin the healing of our minds. In so doing, we are told that we are likely to experience greater peace and joy, less stress, fewer complications and a deeper experience of love—not bad rewards for simply accepting what seems, at least at first, to be an impossible premise. A little willingness, not even faith, is asked of us. We do not have to believe it completely. Faith comes with experience. Being very practical, the Course is designed to lead its students to a first-hand experience of the truth. All that is needed is that we be willing to give it a try.

The Wholeness of God

Despite the many wonderful prayers found throughout the text, and in particular, in Part II of the Workbook, the Course hardly talks about the nature of God, even pointing out that it is impossible for minds that seemingly exist in a state of duality to even begin to understand a God of perfect oneness. Instead, we are given glimpses of what an experience of God might resemble: joy, the absence of fear, certainty, peace of a lasting kind, eternal life, all-encompassing love and unchanging wholeness. God's Love knows no bounds. God's Love is whole, and so what God creates must also be whole.

But to us, whose experience is limited and bound by our identification as separate selves in distinct bodies, perfect oneness is not a concept that can be easily understood. In fact, perfect oneness is not meant to be understood, because the separated mind can only understand separation; it is meant to be felt. This is why Jesus asks us to seek only the experience and to not let theology delay us. To experience separation, in other words, to limit our perception to a unique self that is separate from God, our Creator, a self that has a body, a name and a function in the world, is to give up our true holiness—wholeness. Wholeness cannot know separateness, boundaries or differences; separateness cannot know wholeness. To embrace the Love of God is to relinquish our hold on our belief in a separated self; tall order indeed for the staunch, self-directed, wilful individualists that we are!

Holiness is the acceptance of our innate wholeness as God created us, a state that is complete, indestructible, all-encompassing and eternal. It is attained by relinquishing the wilfulness that is separate from the Will of the Father; it is the only true freedom. To experience true holiness means to say no to judgment because judgment implies differences; true holiness sees that my brother's interests are not separate from my own; true holiness is free of all fear, for what is whole cannot be harmed in any way. True holiness is not fooled by the distractions of the world. The holy are free of the stain of specialness, for to cling to specialness is to foster differences and hierarchies and thus, separation. Guided by the Wisdom of the Father, they hold no grievances, they are patient and understanding, their actions are kind and selfless, and their love reflects the Love of God in its all-inclusiveness. To the truly holy, only one goal is worthy of the Child of God: the experience of the perfect oneness of God and His creations. Nothing else matters; nothing else needs to be done. They gladly come unto their God with wholly empty hands.

Hope for the Non-Holy

Then there is the rest of us, the seemingly non-holy, whose first thoughts of the day were most likely concerned with more mundane issues such as getting that first cup of coffee, sorting out which day of the week it was, waking the kids, checking text messages, matching socks to trousers or getting to work on time. Our first thought was probably not of God. Though well-intentioned and no doubt sincere in our desire to live a "spiritual life," these thoughts indicate that our priorities lie elsewhere.

For the sake of honesty, simplicity and expediency, given that our first thought of the day was probably about something other than of God, let's just say that we stand among the "non-holy" or, more optimistically, the "not yet holy." We may have woken up feeling refreshed and content, perhaps the sun was shining and we looked forward to greeting another day. Or, perhaps we woke up feeling miserable and depressed because something terrible happened at work the day before and we dreaded the consequences to come in the day ahead; or maybe we simply didn't want to get up and slog through yet another dull day in an increasingly sombre life. The following day we may wake up and find that the tide has changed and the sun has stopped shining, and we feel gloomy, or, the storm has passed and we are once again hopeful. And so on throughout our lives. There are good days and there are bad days.

Overall though, life isn't that bad; actually, most of the time it's pretty good, so we think. We've learned to cope and make a decent life for ourselves. In all likelihood, in all our days, rarely, if ever, was our mind on God. We have no idea that the passing pleasures and triumphs, the tiny crumbs of happiness we hold dear, are nothing in comparison to the complete joy we might experience should we learn to remove the barriers to an experience of the truth. Having abandoned our wholeness, we have settled for so very little. How could God's children have anything less than perfect and lasting abundance, joy and peace?

> You cannot walk the world apart from God, because you could not be without Him. He is what your life is. Where you are He is. There is one life. That life you share with Him. Nothing can be apart from Him and live.

"Who walks with me?" This question should be asked a thousand times a day, till certainty has ended doubting and established peace. (W-pI.156.2:4–9; 8:1–2)

A Course in Miracles is a spirituality for the non-holy. It is equally a spirituality for the non-spiritual and the non-religious. To be holy means to uncover and to accept wholeness, to say no to separateness, to be devoid of the desire for specialness and to know that what we perceive as this world is not whole, and therefore cannot be holy. Since we are all created the same, perfectly whole and never lacking for anything, the only thing that distinguishes the seemingly non-holy from the truly holy is curiosity. The truly holy have questioned, they have looked and they have chosen to see that what God created cannot be other than perfectly whole. Being created the same, true holiness is the natural condition of each and every one of us. If this is not our experience, then we must be seeing incorrectly; the solution is to correct the way we look.

In *A Course in Miracles*, Jesus explains to us why we believe ourselves to be anything but holy, how we came to that belief and how to correct what amounts to little more than an erroneous belief. It is a spirituality for those who wish to experience their inherent wholeness, those who seek an experience of the Oneness of God. The Course itself is not holy, nor will reading it make you holy; it will however teach you how you can get in touch with that part of the mind where you can, if you so choose, make that decision for yourself.

The Return of the Ego

If you thought that just because I survived a trek through the desert (the writing of *Leaving the Desert*) that the ego had somehow magically vanished and relinquished its hold on my mind, let me set the record straight. The thought system of the ego remains with us as long as we choose to identify with a self that is separate from perfect oneness. If I'm still writing, chances are that I probably still identify with my self as a writer. That may one day change; but for now, let's just say that I am, just like you, engaged in a slowly evolving process of healing and waking from the dream. With a radical teaching such as *A Course in Miracles*, taking it slowly is not a bad idea. In fact, it's the only way to go, otherwise, the ego's slick, subtle thoughts of specialness can easily slip by the sentinels of our awareness.

You may be wondering if I experienced any resistance while writing this book, perhaps manifesting itself in an uncontrollable urge to make muffins. Not so; at least, not at first. I was quite eager to move forward with it. Even so that, as my muffin supply ran out, I was content to eat leftover pizza for breakfast. Nothing would keep me from writing; readers were waiting for another book. Was there pain in my back and shoulders? Some. But I found a very comfortable position for writing, with feet up on the desk and keyboard on my lap. Not very elegant, but certainly quite comfortable.

However, not long after having written the first couple of chapters, I got stuck. Seriously stuck. Not an ideal situation for a writer to face. I had managed to work some free time into my schedule with the hope of getting some writing done. Writing came after consults and whatever other business needed to be attended to, so any spare time was always very welcome. But I was suffering from a serious case of writer's block. There was an outline and enough topics for a book and, with a few chapters already well underway, I was eager to write, but I had, for some inexplicable reason, been stopped dead in my tracks.

This had never happened before, so I decided to simply go with it. Stressing over what had to be a temporary case of writer's block would not lead to unblocking, it would make it more real than it needed to be. Instead, I spent time in the garden, mowed the lawn, cleaned the house, all the while feeling a mix of confusion over my unusual condition, and some guilt for not having taken advantage of the allotted time to write. However, having grown much less obsessive than in the past—a clear benefit of working with the

Course—and also less attached to my worldly activities, I simply concluded that perhaps I did not need to write this book. After all, the Course does say that I need do nothing. Besides, it's not like writing paid the bills. I had probably said enough with my previous two books anyways. If the urge to write arose again, I could always work on the cookbook I had begun months ago that now sat idling on the hard drive of my computer. Not giving it any more thought, I simply gave it up to the Holy Spirit.

But wait just a minute; I'm nobody's fool. With over six years of intensive work with the Course, you have to get up pretty early to hold me hostage to such a blatant ego manoeuvre. The following morning I awoke with a very clear picture of what had happened: I had, in effect, allowed the ego to take charge of my writing. I forgot to write with the Holy Spirit.

Huh!

Just be normal and write like you normally would, my inner guidance reminded.

Though I had stated in the Introduction that my intention had been to write in my usual, personal style, I had, in fact, not done so. If anything, I had shifted the style ever so slightly, just enough to remove, as much as possible, any sense of "I" from the writing. The ego-identified part of my mind had inserted itself into my writing and attempted to make me sound holy.

Then it's no longer you.

Right! Nice try!

You might think I would have been upset with myself for this blatant ego flare-up, but instead, I found it hilarious. I was still chuckling as I checked my email that morning only to read a message from someone who was reading my books and pointed out that she was enjoying the personal quality of the writing.

Share from personal experience.

The ego had cleverly hijacked my writing and attempted to suppress the self that could share. Having forgotten to write with the Holy Spirit, I had allowed myself to be convinced that there would be no need for personal stories in this book. If there were no personal stories to share, then it would appear as though there was no longer a self, in which case, only holiness remained—well, the illusion of holiness, that is.

And so it was that in the days that followed, I joined with the Holy Spirit and reinserted my "self" into the writing. I wanted true holiness; not a pretend holiness. Obviously, to my ego's profound chagrin, there would be a few more stories to tell, which meant more learning, more mistakes, more forgiveness opportunities, more looking at the obstacles that stood in the way of peace, and ultimately, an experience of the truth. It looked like we were heading back to the old drawing board. School clearly was not yet out.

Starting at the Bottom of the Ladder

The Course uses the ladder as a symbol of both our descent into separation and our journey home. But a ladder has two ends and we must decide which will be our goal; one cannot aim for both ends of a ladder at the same time. At one end is the perfect oneness of God, our true home, that which is real; it is our natural, unchanged, eternal condition. Only our willingness to know it is required. At the other end of the ladder is our belief in what can never be, a seeming state of separation from perfect oneness, a dream self in a dream world experiencing all manner of complicated challenges and situations in a dream life, an unnatural condition which can only be maintained with tremendous effort. Separation is a belief to which we cling furiously and is the result of a choice, just as oneness is experienced by choice.

> What waits in perfect certainty beyond salvation is not our concern. For you have barely started to allow your first, uncertain steps to be directed up the ladder separation led you down. The miracle alone is your concern at present. Here is where we must begin. And having started, will the way be made serene and simple in the rising up to waking and the ending of the dream. (T-28.III.1:1–5)

The Ladder of Separation

The ladder portrays the seeming distance between two distinct points and the steps to be taken in order to travel from one end to the other. The distance too is illusory, but it will feel real to the extent that we are resistant to the thought that we have never left home. As long as we prefer to cling to our separated existence, there appears to be great distance between our experience as a separated self in a body and our true condition of perfect wholeness. The idea of taking steps, especially little steps, can ease some of the overwhelming fear that would otherwise be stirred up should the process be rushed. To the separated self, the return home appears as a very real process, not one to be taken lightly. In truth, the ladder too is part of the dream, and exists only as long as we continue to sustain our belief in separation.

To the truly holy, there is no ladder, there is only the knowledge of God and the perfect oneness of all of His creations. *Stop talking about going home. Know that you are home. This is the miracle.* To the holiness-challenged, if we are ever going to know that we are home, the best place to start is where we believe ourselves to be: at the bottom of the ladder, in bodies, experiencing life as seemingly separated selves. At least now we know there is a ladder, and we know where to find it: in our minds.

Not long after becoming aware that I had chosen the wrong writing partner, it occurred to me that there was nothing that I really needed to do, at least so far as writing was concerned. Writing was part of my healing process, but, the Course tells us, the world was over long ago, and we are just watching reruns of old stories, variations on the one crazy mad idea of separation, and so the healing has already occurred. All I needed was to accept the truth: that I am whole, that you are whole. All we need is to remember the truth. All that is needed is to listen to the right Teacher; take Jesus' hand and let him lead the way.

I get it! It was all so very clear. I cried as I sat at my desk, letting this understanding sink into all levels of my being. I get it! We do not need to make ourselves holy, nor suffer or sacrifice anything in order to attain this holiness. We are already holy! How could we be otherwise? We are as God created us. We only need remember it. That's all. There is nothing to do but to look and see and accept! Really! What greater goal could there possibly be? To set this as our goal is to embrace our inherent holiness. With God as our goal, the end of the journey is certain. With God as our goal, the climb up the ladder is filled with promise, hope and joy! Now, all we need is an experience of this knowledge. This is the beginning of the journey home, the relinquishing of our identification with our false selves in bodies, the uncovering of the knowledge of our selves as minds that have the power to make a different choice.

Let me remember that my goal is God.

Chapter 2

KNOCKING DOWN HEAVEN'S GATE

God's world is happy. Those who look on it can only add their joy to it, and bless it as a cause of further joy in them. We wept because we did not understand. But we have learned the world we saw was false, and we will look upon God's world today. (W-pII.301:2:1–4)

*I*T HAD BEEN A very busy start to the new year, with days and evenings filled with all the many tasks—not to mention the steep learning curve—involved in releasing the digital versions of my books. All of this was over and above the usual new year workshops, seminars and consultations. I had been slowly making my way through the middle of the Workbook Lessons, lingering over those passages which remind us of the truth of our oneness with God. I thought about Brother Lawrence, whom I had come to consider as my favourite symbol of true holiness.

From the young age of eighteen, he realized that all that mattered was to seek to be in the presence of God, remaining loyal to that thought, clinging to it no matter what happened in his life, until his very last day. He was for me a truly holy man, and as a non-holy person myself, I felt inspired by the strength of his conviction and the absolute simplicity of his belief. I thought about the ever-growing complexity of the contemporary world in which we live, the world in which I appear to walk a while. In my heart, I knew that Brother Lawrence had walked in the way of truth, something

I admired deeply, something for which I longed, for there is no worthier quest than to seek to be in the presence of God. Yet this was a state which I felt was still far beyond my reach.

One evening after shutting down the computer and preparing to go to sleep I contemplated the truth of our oneness with God, the fact that this world cannot possibly be our true home, and in particular, that going home and being with God must be much closer at hand than I believed. If this dream was little more than a wisp of cloud hiding the truth, then this dream was nothing. I thought about the insignificance of all the things in and of the world, its intrinsic valuelessness, and how everything in it is so fragile and impermanent. Then I thought of God and my true home in Heaven. There was no worthier goal. Everything else disappeared as I lay my head down on the pillow and pulled the blankets up against the chilly night air. As I contemplated this one simple, uncomplicated thought, I was enveloped by a sense of total and complete peace, safety and wholeness. Overwhelming joy and freedom filled every fibre of my being. There was nothing in this world I wanted more than to be home with God. Everything else paled in comparison to this one thought. It was in the arms of this complete peace and wholeness that I drifted off to sleep.

Since going home is a process—a seemingly lengthy process of undoing the powerful belief in the impossible—I was not surprised at all when, deep into the darkness of that holy night, I found myself trapped in an overwhelmingly disturbing nightmare, the details of which I have absolutely no recollection. All I know is that its images were disturbing enough to pull me out of sleep into the safety of the waking state. Clearly, this business of being in close proximity to God was not looked on very favourably by the part of my mind that still believed in the ego. Life would continue as an inconvenient interlude, until the time I had grown beyond the fear that kept me from my goal.

Going home was my goal. There was no doubt about that; there was nothing that could supplant this sublime desire. This thought alone is what brought me the greatest joy. It is the one thought that gave me the courage and the strength to turn my attention inwards, to uncover the oftentimes not very flattering, and decidedly non-holy motivations behind my every thought and action. Knowing that home was attainable by whomever would turn over his or her life to the Holy Spirit for the purpose of learning to make a different choice made every experience worthwhile.

Stop talking about going home. Know that you are home. This is the miracle.

I thought about Lisa's words frequently, but still, I didn't feel any closer to my goal. Or, perhaps it was more likely that devious part of my wrong mind that refused to accept their truthfulness. However, always the practical mystic, erring on the side of caution, I refused to entertain illusions about my impending holiness and so took that to mean that I would need to set realistic short-term goals for my journey. There would be many small steps before I was ready to take the one, final, smallest of steps to the home I never really left, a step that would not even be taken by me. That part did not belong to me; my job was to do the work that would allow me to meet the conditions of the Kingdom, the first being a peaceful mind, and the second being the relinquishment of all unforgive-ness towards my brothers. Forgiveness was the only worthwhile function. These principles were straightforward and accessible, and above all, very simple, though not always easy to put into practice. Since the tiniest spot of darkness would keep me from my goal, my primary occupation was to be vigilant for my thoughts.

Clearly, I had my work cut out for me, but I remained hopeful, and above all, over the brief six years I had worked with *A Course in Miracles*, I had gained complete trust in, and respect for, the pro-cess. This spirituality was uncompromising and so I must be just as uncompromising in my practice. My commitment to this journey had rewarded me with a more peaceful, joyful life. How could it be otherwise? That which I wanted most was there, accessible to me for when I was ready to accept it.

With practice, I had come to appreciate that this spirituality really worked, a realization that gave me the greatest comfort. I was becoming adept at recognizing when I had chosen, and sometimes even when I was about to choose, with the wrong teacher. It was a straightforward next step to acknowledging that choosing with the wrong mind did not make me feel peaceful. Peace was clearly the more desirable alternative, not only because it brought me closer to my goal, but also because it made me feel better. I learned to recognize when specialness had gotten in the way, which was quite often; when I had pushed away love, probably even more often; or when I had exercised my judgment muscles and chosen to see differences instead of sameness. I forgave myself; I forgave myself often! I learned to stand down from disagreements, sometimes even agreeing with the other person even if our opinions were diametrically opposed. Shared interests did not necessarily extend to the affairs of the world, which were clearly set up to express differences. What we shared was our common decision to continue to believe in the thought of separation and our common yearning for the Love we believed we had forsaken. Being an expression of the mind, oneness had nothing to do with the world.

All the while, I continued to make my way slowly through the Workbook Lessons, amazed at how much more meaning they held after years of intensive study. I had to admit that the first time through the Workbook, though I had read, and practised as sincerely as I could at the time, I really had no idea of what I was doing. None. None, whatsoever. Clueless would aptly describe my initial experience and understanding of the entire Course. But this had changed significantly, I realized, with some surprise as I now read the Course with a whole new understanding and clarity. I got it. I actually understood what I was reading. That in itself was a miracle!

> Is it not He Who knows the way to you? You need not know
> the way to Him. Your part is simply to allow all obstacles that
> you have interposed between the Son and God the Father to
> be quietly removed forever. God will do His part in joyful

and immediate response. Ask and receive. But do not make demands, nor point the road to God by which He should appear to you. The way to reach Him is merely to let Him be. For in that way is your reality proclaimed as well. (W-pI.189.8:1–8)

While my early years of work with the Course had stirred up fear and surprising resistance, my newly burgeoning understanding brought up an entirely new response. When I read certain passages in the Lessons and the Text, I would be moved to tears. There seemed to be a common theme to the content that triggered these episodes: they were the passages that reinforced the message that wholeness was accessible to everyone—you, me and anyone and everyone who is desirous of returning home. They were the passages that remind us of just how near is the Truth; that the return home rested on our readiness to accept the Atonement.

The return to wholeness was a simple matter of preparing the way to make a different choice, not something that had to be earned over years of gruelling spiritual practice and sacrifice, nor something that depended on God smiling favourably on us once we had shown our worthiness. I was moved by the passages that underscored that nothing needed to be done. For a doer such as myself, this was an important lesson. All that was required was the willingness to set aside all other desires and to replace these with the one willingness to trust in the process that Jesus had given us. Peace, wholeness, holiness are our natural condition. It was the passages that remind us that the battle was over long ago, that it never even really began and that it could be released, right now, if and when we desired it so, that brought up the tears.

Following his "Awakening," Ramana related how he had experienced many bouts of "outpouring of the soul in tears… tears that marked this overflow of the soul did not betoken any particular pleasure or pain." My own tears did not come from pleasure or pain, nor from any clear source of grief. They were tears of surrender, as though lifetimes of holding onto untruth were being released. Sometimes, I cried simply because I realized that I actually understood what I was reading. The presence of the truth of the nearness of God spoke to a part of my mind that was quickening in readiness of its acceptance, a presence so great and so welcoming that it caused me to weep in complete and joyful acceptance.

I thought of calling Ken Wapnick for his words of wisdom on the matter, but I was afraid I would cry. I was not a crier. I didn't *do* tears. I even had a script rehearsed for when I would call him, which went something like this: *So, all I need is to pay attention to my mind, identify which teacher I have chosen, the right mind, or the wrong mind, note how I feel and decide to choose otherwise. I get that part. When I choose wrongly, I forgive myself, give it to the Holy Spirit, and let it go. I really need do nothing, since I am reviewing a script that has already happened. My choice for either the right mind or for the wrong mind will determine how my script will play itself out. I get that part too. It is all really simple.* I would continue with my imaginary conversation with Ken, *But there is one more step, right? And that is to accept the Atonement for myself. It is there, waiting for me, when I am ready. That's all there is to it, is that right?*

This is the point at which I would get stuck; every time I began to weep. And since I did not want to cry on the phone, I never made that call. At the same time, I was not foolish enough to think that my bouts of tearfulness indicated the attainment of any special awakening on my part. Unlike Ramana, whose soul had given up its hold on the body, there was no question that I still identified very much with my body, chronic pain and stiffness in the back, hips and arms a bleak daily testament to that fact. The tears, I concluded, were perhaps a clearing of the way, a preparation for what was to come, certainly not the end of the journey. It was no doubt the part of me that yearned to go home, the part that believed that separation from perfect oneness had occurred that cried out in pain.

Yet I remained curious to know more about these strange tearful occurrences; call me cynical, but I suspected there must be some ego-involvement lurking behind them somewhere. One thing I had learned was that as my understanding of the Course's message grew, so did the ego's cleverness at finding ways to slip by the increasingly alert sentinel of my mind. I had grown accustomed to looking deep within for clues about the motivations behind my responses and my actions. Yes, I wept out of a deep longing to return home, but was there something else I needed to see?

Days passed as I patiently waited for the insight that would shed light on my experience; I knew it would eventually come. Answers always came when I was ready to accept them. I had been listening to a wonderful Ken Wapnick workshop: The Pathway of *A Course in Miracles*: from Spirituality to Mysticism, during which bits and pieces of understanding were taking shape. In this workshop, Ken discusses how we choose our life script much like we might choose to watch a movie. Depending on the ego's fiendish proclivities, a person might perhaps enjoy themes of abandonment, and so their life presents them with situations in which they are abandoned by parents, spouses and other loved ones. Another ever popular theme is that of victimization. One can always find something or someone out there that is the cause of our unhappiness, or discomfort, from our genetics to those we once professed to love.

I thought of the themes of my life script as they might relate to my tearing up every time I read a message of hope in my chosen spirituality, and it was not long before I saw what was happening. A long string of past life scenarios unfurled before my mind's eye, the common theme being one of not being quite good enough. I wept at these statements because part of me had accepted the belief that I could never reach home. One quest after another had proven that I was not spiritual enough, not holy enough, not deserving enough of entering the gates of Heaven. Heaven was reserved for God's chosen few; certainly not for one such as me. What arrogance to even think that I might be among them!

Huh!

Although intellectually I knew this to be untrue, I had to acknowledge that this was a belief I harboured, if not consciously, then at least it had been buried deeply in my mind. And it made sense when I looked back at my current life: always second or third, never first. Never the teacher, always the student. Only priests can talk to God; only men can be priests. Although I had long outgrown any desire to be first, famous or foremost, I understood this to be part of the script of my life. Though it did not find an outlet in the world of form, it did find expression in my quest for wholeness.

You can never be holy, the ego sniped back in its defence. *You've never been more than a second-rate monk; you're just another seeker, forever trapped in the never-ending cycle of seeking and not finding. You have a track record of lifetime after lifetime of never having quite what it took for the gates of Heaven to be opened to you; you certainly aren't going to make it with this outrageous big blue book. Who do you think you are? Really!*

> We lay aside the arrogance which says that we are sinners, guilty and afraid, ashamed of what we are; and lift our hearts in true humility instead to Him Who has created us immaculate, like to Himself in power and in love. (W-pI.152.9:4)

Upon realizing this one might think that I would have cried; but I didn't. Well, just a bit when this chapter came up for editing and review. Instead, I had to laugh. It was so silly, so absurd a belief that how could I do anything but laugh! The Course makes it clear that to think anything less of ourselves is arrogance; not the other way around. How could a God of love erect gates between His children and their home? It is impossible. It can only be that Heaven has no gates.

Chapter 3

BEWARE THE SLIGHT TWINGE OF ANNOYANCE

The anger may take the form of any reaction ranging from mild irritation to rage. The degree of the emotion you experience does not matter. You will become increasingly aware that a slight twinge of annoyance is nothing but a veil drawn over intense fury. (W-pI.21.2:3–5)

*L*IFE HAD TAKEN ON a whole new meaning as I became very sensitive to the fact that every single situation, seemingly great or small, was an opportunity to take one step closer toward my goal of awakening from the dream of separation. I was learning to live with a unique, perhaps even unusual, thought system that has nothing to do with the world in which I live, a process that left me feeling at times divided and even confused. Since the ego is not about to go down without a fight, as might be expected, my growing faith in my new life direction and purpose ignited a battle for survival between the right and wrong parts of my mind, the battleground of choice being my body. Casualties of war included my back, shoulders, neck, ribs, arms, wrists, hips, and, if I poked around some, I'd find painful spots in my legs too. Needless to say, I looked forward to the day when my soul, like Ramana's, would give up its hold on the body.

As much as I understood that ultimately, healing was of the mind, I also understood that I needed to take care of the body, for it was, after all, an integral part of the classroom of my life. I resumed yoga practice and focused on stretching and flexibility. Still stuck at the beginner level and certainly not a picture of grace, the stretching did help alleviate some of the discomfort. But more importantly, I realized that I was no longer afraid of the quiet. I was well aware that I had consciously avoided yoga practice over the winter months because it brought me too close to the quiet in my mind. Yoga is for me a time of peaceful surrender, by far not a condition that is conducive to the maintenance and survival of the ego. One does not have to be spiritually enlightened to see that the world is a very noisy place, nor does it appear as though it will get quieter any time soon. From the perspective of the ego, noise is good; quiet is bad. With my growing attraction for the peace of God, quiet would certainly be perceived as an undesirable state. But now, I looked forward to the quiet and the stretching, and made it a priority in my daily schedule, something I saw as progress, indicating that my fear of getting in touch with the long-hidden decision-making part of my mind was beginning to wane.

Do You Really Want the Peace of God?

Naturally, in order for learning to become real, it must be experienced directly. It's one thing to have a grasp of the theory, even an excellent grasp, it's a whole other matter when it comes to applying it to the specifics of everyday life. Without application, it remains little more than theory; perhaps fancy, sophisticated and even inspiring theory, but theory nonetheless. Eager to apply what I had been learning, I accepted an invitation from a client to the opening of a new alternative health clinic where she taught yoga. Although I frequently received invitations to a wide variety of events, often working nights, and generally preferring a quiet existence, I accepted very few. However, always on the lookout for good practitioners for myself as well as referrals for my clients, I shuffled my schedule around and accepted the invitation. Since my mom was looking for a good osteopath, I invited her to join me.

It was a beautiful clinic, with dark wood floors, subdued lighting and limited furnishings; very Zen, a minimalistic look that appealed very much to my sense of simplicity. I spoke with my client, the two young osteopaths and a podiatrist. I chatted with each specialist, seeking to learn more about their approaches, thinking that perhaps I might find someone who might help with my back issues.

This may sound strange coming from someone who mixed cough syrups from herbs and healed her daughters with her hands but, in my experience, I had not known much success with many alternative practitioners, in particular, those who were overly spiritual or "alternative." I have met many health practitioners—traditional and alternative—through my practice, and know, for a fact, that most are just as broken and just as sad and just as empty inside as the next person, sometimes even more so, since many were attracted to the healing arts in order to heal themselves. As a practical person, I preferred the more hands on, move-things-into-place approaches.

The people who worked in this lovely new clinic, I was told, were all very spiritual. But that was okay, as I understood well the culture of the alternative practices. They needed to create an environment that inspired healing, also, one that would inspire people to pay the hundred dollars for their treatments, I told myself as I moved on as non-judgmentally as I could to meet the Thai yoga massage therapist. Which is where I encountered the real purpose of my outing that evening: to test my willingness to continually choose with the right mind.

You say you want the peace of God? Really? Let's just see how much you really want it! The ego taunted, never far afield, and if I hadn't been so busy trying to be in my right mind, I would have seen it chomping at the bit, just waiting for an opportunity to invite me to lose it. So far, I had done rather well, managing to overlook judgmental thoughts as best I could, listening with an open mind to the many ways in which these wonderfully gifted people could heal another person's body. Soon, I would go home and this whole ordeal would be over.

Another guest at the event, a younger woman who had been standing by as I chatted with the massage therapist chimed into our conversation with a cheery and very, okay—overly enthusiastic, bordering on annoying—discourse on the importance of looking at the blockages in the body and beaming energy from the mind so that the blockages could be removed. She picked up a whole whack of New Age steam as she began to lecture on energy blockages, including the blockages in the energy in *my* back and how I should look inside to see what was blocking me and then beam energy from my mind, and when she stressed how she knew all about what was going on in *my* body, I burst out laughing, and, with the utmost restraint and as pleasantly as I could, I said, "You don't know the first thing about what's going on in my body." As self-appointed master of my own misguided destiny, I certainly wasn't about to take advice from some flaky New Age fanatic! We let it go at that, and laughed, the steam was gone from the discourse, and when she saw my business card and asked if I had written all the books displayed on the back, I answered, yes, those were some of them, hence the tightness in the back and arms.

The entire situation probably appeared innocuous on the surface, but it rattled me. It bugged me for days. I looked at it with Jesus, acknowledging that I had clearly expressed some defensiveness, and hence lost my sense of peace. Instead of simply letting her go on with her sermon, and acknowledging her passion for her beliefs, I had reacted defensively. She wasn't a practitioner and she wasn't about to extract a hundred dollars from me; she just wanted to be heard. She felt the need to convince herself that she knew something of importance about energy and healing, and that was her issue, not mine, but I had made it mine. If I had remained right-minded, I might simply have nodded or agreed with her, or if she seemed to expect a response, I might have acknowledged her enthusiasm for her studies and said something like: Wow, you really love what you do! But I didn't; instead, I had become defensive. The switch had been flipped and I knew with whom I danced: the dark partner of defensiveness.

Despite what might have been considered justifiable annoyance with the energy-beaming woman, because I remained bothered by the situation, I had to admit that something she said must have rung a bell, otherwise, it would have rolled right over me like water off a duck. Having grown increasingly appreciative of the peaceful state of mind, I had also grown particularly sensitive to its loss, and, unable to fully reclaim my peace of mind, I thought about the matter a whole lot over the week that followed. As much as I tried to convince myself that I had responded kindly by making a joke of the situation, I remained upset for having lost my peace and was clearly annoyed by something she had said.

> When the ego tempts you to sickness do not ask the Holy Spirit to heal the body, for this would merely be to accept the ego's belief that the body is the proper aim of healing. Ask, rather, that the Holy Spirit teach you the right *perception* of the body, for perception alone can be distorted. Only perception can be sick, because only perception can be wrong. (T-8.IX.1:5–7)

In re-examining my attitude regarding my health issues, I came to see that I had approached the situation incorrectly. Sincerely believing to be doing the right thing, I had given it up to the Holy Spirit: The Holy Spirit will take it away when I don't need it any more. This had been my attitude. Though an attitude of surrender is not an evil thing, in this case, it was destined to not bring me the results I sought. In hindsight, I realized that this was perhaps not the wisest approach. It was not working. Instead, I was learning to live with pain. Instead of looking for the origin of my discomfort, a decision made in my mind, I had handed over the responsibility of healing to the Holy Spirit. It was not the Holy Spirit that was making my body ill; it was me. This is what I needed to look at.

I was still listening to the same Ken Wapnick workshop: The Pathway of *A Course in Miracles*: from Spirituality to Mysticism, when something triggered my attention inwards and made me take a closer look. This is when I saw it: the deep, dark, sickly self-loathing. The pain in my body was an expression of the self-hatred that lay buried deep in my mind.

The following morning I awoke with the very clear decision: this had to stop now. I was about to turn fifty-seven and I felt like I was a hundred and fifty-seven. This was not right. It had to stop. Clearly, I had become the victim of my deeply repressed self-hatred which was oozing out and being projected onto my body. This was silly and it had to stop! I scheduled an appointment with Mrs Hong, a Chinese doctor I had seen a couple of times during the previous year.

As I lay on the table in Mrs Hong's clinic, I thought of the lesson on the *Course in Miracles* flip calendar on the shelf that caught my attention on the way out of the house that morning: I choose the joy of God instead of pain. Very hands-on, Mrs Hong was anything but New Age, alternative or spiritual; I don't know what thoughts she was beaming, but she attacked my back like a butcher pounding a veal cutlet into scaloppini, stuck me with needles and sucked the skin off my back with strange little suction cups that she sealed into place by quickly pumping some moving part. When I returned home, I jumped when I saw my back: a tapestry of deep purple crop circles. I had wanted hands-on. There it was, I laughed. I scheduled weekly sessions with Mrs Hong over the next few weeks, kept up with yoga practice, did some body rolling, as instructed by my daughter, and began the process of really looking. After six years of intensive study, the practical application of the principles of *A Course in Miracles* in my life was actually beginning. Let's do it, I told my teacher. With Jesus by my side, I felt as though I could move a mountain, even the mountain of guilt that stood between me and the Love of God.

Chapter 4

WHERE IS THE LOVE?

> You made the ego without love, and so it does not love you. You could not remain within the Kingdom without love, and since the Kingdom *is* love, you believe that you are without it. (T-6. IV.2:3–4)

Nothing Personal, it's Just 100% Hate

SINCE IT APPEARED THAT my ego clearly was not overly thrilled with, nor was it about to cooperate with my desire for extended periods of peaceful grace, I decided to take a closer look at how it works. Peace is not something that can be faked; only the peace of God—peace of a lasting kind—would get me home. Any form of conflict whatsoever, even the tiniest thought of resentment or impatience, was sufficient to keep me from that goal. The best approach, I gathered, was to know my enemy well.

The thought system of the ego is one hundred percent hate, while the Holy Spirit's is one hundred percent love, Ken Wapnick reminds us—all too often, if you ask my ego-identified self. Since the premise of *A Course in Miracles* is pure non-dualism, the two thought systems must be mutually exclusive, which means they cannot exist both at the same time, and so when we choose one, the other disappears. Until taught otherwise, we remain unaware of the fact that we are constantly choosing between one thought system or the other, something we are doing every moment of every day. Everything we experience is a result of our choosing. When we commit to a choice, the outcome of that choice partakes of the nature of that choice. To change an outcome requires that we make a different choice. By the same token, the outcome of a situation reveals quite clearly which choice we have made. If we experience joy, love, sharing, it must be because we have chosen to join with another; if we experience conflict, it must be because we have chosen to push away love.

> You may wonder why it is so crucial that you look upon your hatred and realize its full extent. You may also think that it would be easy enough for the Holy Spirit to show it to you, and to dispel it without the need for you to raise it to awareness yourself.... You could look even upon the ego's darkest corner-stone without fear if you did not believe that, without the ego, you would find within yourself something you fear even more. You are not really afraid of crucifixion. Your real terror is of redemption. (T-13.III.1:1–2; 9–11)

For those of us whose experience is one of separateness from perfect oneness, for whom another level of mind seems like at best, a vague, remote, esoteric concept, at worst, something we believe that, due to our inherent unworthiness, we could never attain, the idea of making a different choice seems nearly impossible. Since there are only two alternatives, the matter is greatly simplified; we can choose either love, or hate, not both, not neither, not anything in between nor some alternative mash-up of the two. Being mutually exclusive, there can be no love in a decision based on hate, and hate does not exist when love has been chosen. We cannot bring a little bit of love in a decision based on hate any more than a woman can be a little bit pregnant. In fact, the Course says that what is not love is murder.

Among its many fascinating talents, fuelled by a deep fear of love, the ego breeds defensiveness, specialness, judgment, competition, hierarchies, scarcity—all themes that are based on differences and lack of wholeness and which reflect the need to protect itself from the belief that what God created is vulnerable to, and even deserving of, attack and punishment. This means that as long as we choose with a thought system that keeps us from our wholeness, as long as we cling to our very special unique "self," separate and distinct from our brothers, everything we think and do cannot come from love. As long as we choose hate, we keep away the one thing we long for the most: the Love of God.

Under the spell of an imagined separated state, we cannot even truly love ourselves, for love, which is a reflection of oneness and wholeness, is impossible in a mind that adheres to a belief in separation. The self-love of the separated soul is really love of the ego, which is born of a thought of hate, which means then that it is not love at all, but rather self-loathing in disguise. Much of what passes for love in this world is little more than a paltry substitute for the Love of God, a cover for the fear of love that lies at the pit of the ego's thought system.

Love hurts, a rejected lover will proclaim, confusing the intensity of his pain of rejection with love. Love does not hurt; love cannot hurt. What he is feeling is a mix of anger, resentment, grief and sadness over having lost the object of his desire, the object of his so-called love being perceived as little more than a possession. Some seem to think that the more they suffer or grieve over the loss of a loved one, the more love they must have felt. Since Love created us whole, and Love is eternal and unalterable, Love cannot be lost. It simply is.

What we are motivated or guided to do from this separated condition serves only the purpose of nurturing and sustaining separation from our Source, from the Love that is our natural inheritance. This unnatural state we work hard at maintaining can only be expressed as some form of tension, defensiveness, struggle or conflict. The ego does not have our best interests at heart, it does not serve to make us peaceful or whole, and it certainly does not support our search for the true meaning of love. In all ways and in all circumstances, the ego serves only its need to remain the number one choice in our mind. The ego is a thought of hate and the body is perceived as the ego's home. Love is all-encompassing, and therefore cannot be contained in a home that limits and separates; nor can it be controlled, contained or limited in any way. It is not something that is bargained for, traded or exchanged. Love simply is; love allows love to be.

The Ego's Revenge

What I would next experience first-hand is how the body can be used by the ego as a perfect object onto which it can project its hatred. Over the weeks that followed my realization that the pain in my body was most likely connected to the self-loathing I harboured deep inside, I made it a point to be more aware of this hatred, especially when I felt pangs of pain in my back. I knew that ultimately, I must look at the hatred before I could know the love that waits patiently on the other side. I understood that the hatred was a cover-up for the ego's overwhelming fear that I would one day, once and for all, decide in favour of my perfection, and I was okay with that. Looking was part of the process and should not be rushed, but it was also the only way to dispel the erroneous belief in sin and guilt. Looking was necessary; there was no way around it. The love I sought was beyond the hate; the fear that kept it all in place expressed itself as a pain-riddled battle in my body.

Meanwhile, I picked up some homeopathic remedies, took ibuprophen when the pain bothered me too much, stepped up my yoga practice, which consisted mostly of stretching exercises and attended weekly sessions with Dr. Hong. Yoga practice became more enjoyable as I gained strength and flexibility. The Course asks us simply to look. I appreciated very much that we are not asked to analyze, nor try to uncover the connections between our thoughts and our bodies; we are simply asked to look. What would be the point of analzing a thought system that was clearly insane? The ego is a thought of hatred; since I believed myself to be separate from my Source, there must be some hatred there. I kept an eye out for it, without judging myself when I became aware of it, or when my back hurt. It was all so very silly, I reminded myself. Just look, without judgment, Jesus asks of us.

The pain in my back and shoulders began to subside, and I was thrilled when I woke up several mornings in a row relatively pain free. It can't be that easy, I thought to myself. I trusted in the process of healing set forth by the Course, but I also knew that the thought system of the ego would not be undone overnight and I wasn't about to fool myself into an imaginary enlightened state. I wanted the real thing.

The ego wouldn't remain in silent hiding forever; my growing appreciation for peace as the better choice had to stir up some anxiety in the insane netherworld of my mind. It was sure to come out of hiding sooner or later. And it did; like a raging bull it broke out of its pen, hell-bent on destroying all my hard work at undoing the thought system I had decided no longer suited my goal. *Peace, kindness, gentleness! Hell no! That just won't do*, it taunted. *That's way too close to the choice for love. If you won't hate yourself, we'll find someone else to hate.* And it did. Those poor kind, gentle, souls I met that day had no idea of the depth and intensity of the hatred that was catapulted in their direction, their sole crime being that they sold a product that I did not really care for. This was no ordinary projection; it was fierce. In fact, it was so vicious that, not only was the work of Dr. Hong undone and the pain in my back returned, I also became nauseous.

A Time for Faith

While I was drowning in a sea of hatred of my own choosing, my faith in the process of forgiveness became my life jacket, and I clung to it as though my very existence depended on it, knowing that I would eventually return to that peaceful place in my mind. With Jesus as my anchor, I looked at my decision for hatred. It was at the foundation of my specialness, my uniqueness, my separated self.

The entire process took the better part of four days; much longer than I would have liked, but I understood that the healing would take the time I needed to give up a lifelong habit of faulty thinking. The same power to choose wrongly was available for me to choose rightly whenever I was ready. Since time was of the illusion, then, the time to make that choice was now. Each time doubt stirred, I immediately pushed it aside. I was looking without judgment at an insane choice, a choice I hoped to replace in the nearest possible future with a saner choice. This was trial by hatred and I hoped to never again go down that dark, desolate road. However, I accepted that if facing the hatred was necessary in order to uncover the love, I was ready for it, knowing that it would bring me yet again, one step closer to my goal.

As a wrong-minded reaction to what I thought was a tiny step forward on my journey, I felt compelled to punish myself. I had a strong urge to buy a cheesecake, eat the whole thing and make myself sick; I thought of getting drunk and obliterating all sense of self. Naturally, I immediately recognized these thoughts as coming from a terrified ego, facing the slow, steady dismantling of its defence structures, and so I ignored them. Instead, I went for long walks, listened to a Ken Wapnick workshop, practiced yoga, worked in the garden and walked some more, made healthy meals with fresh herbs from the garden and enjoyed a glass of wine with dinner. The thought system of the ego may be insane, but, still in charge of the choices I made, I was not. I didn't have to be a pawn to its self-destructive antics. I watched, and I waited it out, patiently, knowing it was part of the journey, certain that the light awaited on the other side of the darkness.

Staying with the feeling, I placed my entire faith in the process. Just beyond the hate is the love. Jesus asks us to bring the darkness to the light, to bring the hate to the love. Everywhere I looked, I saw opportunities to project hate. It did not matter whether I had known a person a minute, or a lifetime, hate was there, ever ready to be splashed all over whomever I interacted with. The hate was dark, gritty, palpable and very nauseating. So I looked, and watched and listened to inner guidance.

What we believe to be sinful about ourselves is part of the thought system of separation. Go through the hate and self-hate; but, without doing anything about it. Your part is to withdraw your investment in what the mind projects. Deny the denial of truth. Since only love is true, hate, or any other negative emotion must simply be the denial of truth. The only solution is to deny the denial of love. To make the conscious choice to withdraw from the ego's projections is to be in one's right mind. To look without judgment is to join with the Holy Spirit. The ego would not do this. Do nothing now. Have faith in the process that has brought you this far; being a natural process of returning to wholeness, it must inevitably be completed. The love that your self-hate is a defence against will come to the surface and dissolve it.

Had I not been well-versed in the teaching of the Course, motivated by deep-seated guilt and believing myself to be a terrible person, I would most probably have been tempted to cover up this nasty hate fest, deny its existence, find something outside my mind, in the world, to preoccupy me. But I stayed with it until I started to laugh. In time, it just grew incredibly ridiculous. Then I recalled a short video clip produced by the Royal Canadian Airfarce honouring recently deceased comedian Roger Abbott in which he spoofed dark, brooding, singer-songwriter Leonard Cohen:

A mother, a child
A flower, sunshine
I hate them, I hate them, I hate them
A knowing smile
A soft caress
A warm embrace
A lasting kiss
I hate them, I hate them, I hate them

This song became my anthem for the hate of the ego, and I laughed and laughed whenever my ego went into hate mode. On the fifth morning, I awoke with a clear understanding of what had occurred. The self-hatred that had been projected onto my body was not being projected onto me, really, it was nothing personal; hatred is simply what the ego is. The true Self cannot hate or feel hated. The false self does not exist. So where is the hatred? If anger is never justified, so must it be with hatred.

The hatred I had been projecting onto my body was completely unnecessary; it was not even about me or my body. It belonged to an insane, illusory thought system which did not even belong to me, and of which I did not need to be a victim. In fact, I am not the ego; I only believed it was my only choice. True power resides in the mind's ability to choose. Instead, I could choose peace; which I did. In choosing peace, love follows; and it did. And yes, I cried, and I cried, and I cried some more.

> You think you have made a world God would destroy; and by loving Him, which you do, you would throw this world away, which you *would*. Therefore, you have used the world to cover your love, and the deeper you go into the blackness of the ego's foundation, the closer you come to the Love that is hidden there. *And it is this that frightens you.* (T-13.III.4:3–5)

Know Thyself

How do we know whether we have chosen love or hate? Our thoughts, feelings and actions reflect our choices. Love sees no differences, it is kind and peaceful, it is free of judgment, it sees everyone's interests as the same, it recognizes that we are all one, wholly holy, united in our Father, our Source. Love does not breed specialness because it does not see differences; nor does it set its own interests ahead of those of another. It listens with a truly open mind and a forgiving heart, and respects a brother's choices knowing that each brother has the same power to choose. Love does not see two; it sees that we are one. Love knows that there really is nothing that need be done, since the impossible never occurred.

Through my work, I have met countless individuals who have struggled with guilt over the difficulty, and sometimes seeming impossibility, of expressing love and kindness towards those who, they rightly feel are deserving of nothing less. One client expressed how difficult it was for him to get along with his stepdaughter. I pointed out that all she wanted was to be loved and accepted, to which he said nothing. As he was leaving, I suggested that he just give her a very big hug, to which he shrugged and replied, "I just can't do that."

We all know that everyone is deserving of the same love, but how can we express love for a parent or sibling towards whom we harbour deep-seated resentment for some perceived injustice? How can we express love for someone for whom at best, we are able to muster up sufficient self-control to not rip out their hearts with our bare hands? This seeming inability to express love universally almost without fail extends toward ourselves, though we try hard to put on a brave face of self-acceptance and self-understanding.

In our sincerity to be good people, we work hard at being considerate, kind, loving contributing members of the families, communities and societies to which we belong. We smile and are polite, we give of our time and of ourselves, and at the end of the day, we pride ourselves in having been good persons. At least, we didn't go out and shoot anyone today. What we do not realize is that while we practice our slick forms of worldly love, not only are we expending tremendous amounts of our treasured so-called creative energy to find clever ways of forcing down the hatred that is our deeply hidden belief, we are also denying ourselves an experience of the true love for which we so deeply yearn. How could we do otherwise? How could we be truly loving when we are not aware of the fear and the hatred that stand between us and the love that is the very essence of our being? How could we be loving when love is the antidote to the hate that the ego so desperately needs for its survival?

As a preliminary practice, rather than attempting to do what seems at first impossible—to love thyself—it might be wise to *know* thyself. You cannot love what you do not know, and to know some-one or something is to love them. Know how much you fear love. All barriers to love's expression must be looked at, brought to light and then released. This requires a fair amount of willingness and courage, but above all, a sincere desire to rejoin with the love we believe we have traded in for a moment of foolish separation. Learn to recognize those circumstances, the particular interactions with others that cause you, sometimes in the most subtle ways, to push away love.

Love is not taught; it does not require practice, teaching, preach-ing or learning of any sort. Love is not a word, it is not a religion, a spirituality, a book nor is it a teaching. There are no words to describe love; it simply is. Love is the natural extension of what we are, as God created us, and since love is the nature of God, then our nature too, is love. Love created us. Love is known when it is expressed and shared unconditionally with something or someone else. It must be given in order to be recognized. Since love is eternal, it can never be depleted nor lost. To give love through caring for another is to give love a voice, it is to allow it's natural, free expres-sion. Only then can love be known.

> Your task is not to seek for love, but merely to seek and find all of the barriers within yourself that you have built against it. It is not necessary to seek for what is true, but it *is* necessary to seek for what is false. Every illusion is one of fear, whatever form it takes. And the attempt to escape from one illusion into another must fail. If you seek love outside yourself you can be certain that you perceive hatred within, and are afraid of it. Yet peace will never come from the illusion of love, but only from its reality. (T-16.IV.6:1–6)

Chapter 5

A TIME FOR FAITH

Faith and belief and vision are the means by which the goal of holiness is reached. Through them the Holy Spirit leads you to the real world, and away from all illusions where your faith was laid. This is His direction; the only one He ever sees. And when you wander, He reminds you there is but one. His faith and His belief and vision are all for you. (T-21.III.4:1–5)

Too Close for Comfort

*M*OST *COURSE IN MIRACLES* students have reached, or are very likely to eventually reach a point where they slam the book shut, throw it against a wall or out the window, or pass it through the shredder, all the while sending not-so-subtle and perhaps very colourful accusations in the direction of its author. I've been there more than once! Being the author of our dream means that we are responsible for everything that appears to happen to us in the dream, all the good stuff, and, most annoyingly, all the bad stuff. This fact is among the most difficult aspects of the Course's teaching to digest; no one wants to be responsible for the bad stuff in their lives. No one wants to admit to being responsible for their feelings of pain, anguish, depression, anger, resentment, abandonment, injustice, loneliness, grief or disquiet of any kind. It is much easier, and certainly more comforting, to find someone or something to blame for our lack of peace.

The secret of salvation is but this: that you are doing this unto yourself. No matter what the form of the attack, this still is true. Whoever takes the role of enemy and of attacker, still is this the truth. Whatever seems to be the cause of any pain and suffering you feel, this is still true. (T-27.VIII.10:1–4)

When faced with the reality of the role we have played in our own misery, a natural reaction is to turn away. We look for something that will make us feel better, if only for a short time. This is where many students will turn toward other spiritualities as a way of finding solutions to a problem they have made, but would rather forget that they have made, spiritualities that either do not dwell on this point, or overlook it altogether. *A Course in Miracles* takes us to the root of the problem: the mind's decision for separation. It also shows us where to find the solution: seeing that in truth, there is no problem, because separation could never be. The problem and the solution both are found inside the mind. However, even for the bravest of souls, a certain discomfort is bound to arise when a process that is designed to undo everything we believe we are is engaged.

Right from the start, without a moment's hesitation I fully embraced *A Course in Miracles* as the right path for me. This was the teaching I had been searching—and preparing—for all my life. I jumped right in, frankly not really knowing what I was getting myself into, for such is my nature. Being a confirmed "doer," I tend to throw myself wholeheartedly into projects and interests, figuring out a plan as I stumble forward. It is an approach that has had its share of hits, as well as misses, but it is the approach with which I am familiar. With over half a century of practice, why change now!

In a way, it is a blessing that I was clueless as to the full depth and power of the teaching of the Course, for, had I known what it really entailed—that I would have to face the deeply hidden role I played in my own lack of peace, I think I might have been scared off. It wasn't long before I realized that it would take a bit of time to acquire a sufficient grasp of the Course's metaphysics—I know, a lot of time, a minor glitch for an impatient person such as myself—for there was no way I could even begin to apply this teaching in the ordinary situations of my life without a solid understanding of its essential principles. And without application, there would be no real learning. Despite the initial learning curve, not once did it occur to me to look for another path. I was in it for the long haul; Jesus was stuck with me as a student, and I had no problem being in the slow class. He would match his infinite patience to my resolute—bordering on obsessive—determination. Bring it on; I can do this, was my battle cry on the journey home.

For the first few years, I must admit that I found it almost impossible to actually apply the messages of the Course in my everyday life. The radical notion that the world is an illusion, an outside picture of an inward condition, was not very helpful in addressing the overwhelming non-illusory stuff of life in an overly noisy and busy world, nor did it pay the non-illusory bills piled up on my desk, although nothing would have given me more pleasure than to make the bills illusory! There was a normal, regular life to be dealt with and it wasn't going to disappear anytime soon.

I focused on studying and learning the theory of this brand new spirituality without making any heroic attempts at applying it perfectly, all the while forgiving myself when I stumbled, trying not to pile on more guilt when I really fumbled. Meanwhile, I continued to deal with the day-to-day business of life in a body—as well as could possibly be expected, considering this radical new perspective on a made-up life in a made-up world. There was my work with the Course, which included writing, and there were my numerous non-Course activities; and while I plodded along, making sincere attempts at forgiving my brother for what he "had not done," the two planes of existence did not very often intersect.

It was well into my sixth year of work with the Course before I felt that my everyday life was beginning to merge with my spiritual quest. This became most apparent in my writing, where, each time I broached a new chapter or section, usually based on a hunch that this is what had to be written about at the time, the subject of my writing would show up as daily forgiveness and learning opportunities. At first, I was not sure if it was the writing that paralleled what was going on in my life or if it was the writing that prompted parallel experiences.

I had been thinking a lot about the practice of stepping outside the dream with Jesus and just looking, an essential part of working with the Course. Watching myself going about my daily activities, watching as I slipped into my various roles, then pulling back and watching the doer. On one particular day I was pondering the gentle dream that this practice would lead to. What might it be like to live a gentle dream? I had finished running a few errands and was backing the car out of its spot in the nearly empty parking lot. A gentle dream. I liked the sound of that, I pondered as I slowly looked over my shoulder and shifted the car out of reverse and into first. That's when I saw the blue van, parked within inches of my back bumper. I hadn't seen it when I got in the car. Had I been in another frame of mind, impatient, anxious, or thinking about some problem that needed solving in my important world, I very likely would have backed right into it. What I found interesting is that I drove off completely unruffled, as though absolutely nothing had happened. That day, I had chosen to experience peace, and truly meant it; the gentle dream was the result.

I concluded that the most likely explanation for these parallels between my thoughts and events in my life was that, as I was growing increasingly familiar and comfortable with the message of the Course, I was becoming much more in touch with the decision-making power of the mind. At the same time, I was also becoming acutely aware of the mechanics of projection at work in the mind. It became increasingly clear that my experiences as a physical, mental, emotional body living in a complex world, were none other than an outside picture of what resided deeply buried inside my mind. This body, with its experiences that seemed to be occurring outside my mind, was a reflection of, not only what I believed to be true, but even more shockingly, what I *wanted* to be true, for my experiences were not always gentle and peaceful.

> As the light comes nearer you will rush to darkness, shrinking from the truth, sometimes retreating to the lesser forms of fear, and sometimes to stark terror. But you will advance, because your goal is the advance from fear to truth. The goal you accepted is the goal of knowledge, for which you signified your willingness. Fear seems to live in darkness, and when you are afraid you have stepped back. Let us then join quickly in an instant of light, and it will be enough to remind you that your goal is light. (T-18.III.2)

Writing is a deeply introspective, intellectual activity; it places the mental faculties in a logical, analytical mode, at least, this has been this author's experience. When I have completed a block of writing, I customarily give my brain a rest, returning after a day or so, sometimes after a couple of weeks, or longer. The fresh new perspective allows me to flesh out ideas, tighten up content, and generally get started on the editing. While working on this, my seventh book, having grown comfortable with the writing process, I found that I was able to toggle between two or three sections at a time, sometimes in no particular order, something my linear-thinking brain would have been unable to accomplish when I first began to write. This allowed for a broader and more intense study of the material, as I could approach it from several angles at the same time.

One might think that writing might stimulate inspiration and increased understanding, and to a certain extent, it does. However, it is really during the quiet times that inspiration arises, usually upon waking in the morning, or, unfortunately for someone who appreciates her good night's sleep, in the middle of the night, when the mind is free of thinking and senseless analysis. This in itself was a big clue as to the nature and purpose of thinking, a lesson I would soon learn, one that would serve to remove a huge barrier to the truth.

Since the purpose of *A Course in Miracles* is to lead its students to a new way of thinking, this intense immersion in a program of study designed to undo the thought system of the ego was bound to stir up the cauldron of fear, and so it was not surprising that during those periods when I spent a lot of time writing, at some point, the ego stuff would hit the fan. Then as soon as I returned to the safety of the mundane, like the spoiled child that it was, the ego would settle down, as though breathing a sigh of relief, reassured that its position as most-cherished thought system remained intact.

After setting aside the first draft of the chapter on hate, which, surprisingly, I had much fun writing and, more importantly, survived relatively unscathed, I moved on to work on the recap of the myth of separation, taking yet one more look at the dreaded story of sin, guilt and fear. My ego never liked it when I went there, immediately pointing my attention toward worldly distractions such as checking email, updating my website, pulling weeds from flower beds, doing laundry, and yes, even baking the occasional batch of muffins—anything to keep my mind focused outward. I suppose I was pressing my luck a bit because, at the same time, I also prepared a seminar on Special Relationships, yet another favourite ego subject, which I tied into the hate that always lurks behind the ego's declarations of special love. It was inevitable that at some point, this highly potent cocktail would cause the ego to raise an angry objection. There were only two possible outcomes: an expression of the fear that I might actually take this *Course in Miracles* teaching seriously or, peace, stemming from a quiet recognition of the truth. It would be one or the other; just not both at the same time. That was the way of the split mind.

That's when I experienced the full brunt of the ego's resistance and fear. Actually, it was more like an ambush; obviously, I had been drilling a bit too close to the truth of perfect oneness for the comfort of my separated existence. No doubt feeling threatened by my daily dabbling in a Course designed for the purpose of its undoing, the part of my mind that identified with the ego's thought system of separation had but one recourse: quickly find a clever way to haul my attention out of the quiet depths of my mind and send it back in the world where its safe reign would once again be re-established. *Get that woman out of her mind—pronto!* The ego demanded.

In response to the ego's desperate desire to deflect impending threats to its illusory existence, the perfect opportunity for unloading some deeply rooted guilt and fear came in the form of a message I received from a reader, someone I had known for some time, which contained a rather negative criticism of my last book and of my work with the Course. The ego immediately recognized this situation as chock full of potential for delicious, drawn out, distressing conflict. Still within range of my right mind, my initial reaction was to simply laugh it off; it was all so very silly, and I could simply have left it at that. *Not so fast lady!* A vicious voice from my wrong mind snapped. With a history of differences of opinion, this was, from the perspective of the ego, the perfect set-up and, unable to stay in my right mind—or more accurately, choosing to side in favour of protecting my wounded separated self—I fell for it, lock, stock and barrel. And I fell real hard.

First off, I reminded myself that I was not responsible for this person's sentiments, a fact in which I found only very small comfort. It is very easy to fall into the trap of assuming responsibility for another person's feelings, to feel guilty for being the cause of someone's upset. However, when looked at from the perspective of a teaching that says that each person is responsible for his or her feelings, to assume responsibility for someone's actions or responses is to assume a power that does not belong to us, and is, in fact just another form of the ego's arrogance. Everyone has the power to choose between peace, or conflict, at any time. Still, this knowledge alone was not sufficient to steer me back to my right mind.

While I was not responsible for this person's feelings, I most certainly was responsible for how I perceived the situation, and it was very clear that I had chosen to see it with the dark and distorted lens of the ego. What I saw was an attack, and my initial reaction was to become defensive, and this time, Workbook Lesson 153: "In my defenselessness my safety lies" just wasn't cutting it. The simple, unspiritual fact of the matter was that I felt personally and unjustly attacked and my automatic response was to defend myself. Had I stayed in my right mind long enough, I would have seen it as a call for love, as are all attacks on a brother, or an expression of fear, again, as are all attacks on a brother; instead I saw only an unkind, unjustified attack.

It was my writing and my work with the Course that were under attack; a most important part of my life, as perceived from within a framework of hierarchies of important work. This was a serious attack! Evidently, from the perspective of the ego, my "work" was more important than seeing the call for love that stood behind the encounter, proof positive that I did not really want peace, and love, well, that was certainly not as important as work. Not wanting to engage in conflict and feeling defenceless at the hand of my attacker, I plunged into a sea of self-doubt about my writing and, ultimately, about my work with *A Course in Miracles*. In less time than it takes to say forgiveness, I had lost my precious peace in the face of a perceived injustice. What kind of Course student was I? Maybe this person was right; my spiritual path was completely impractical. Recent experiences of grace and deep peace and an unshakable desire to return to my true home notwithstanding, who was I kidding! Feeling overwhelmed, I prayed to the Holy Spirit to help free me from this horrible darkness and to help me see the situation differently.

Though sincere in my prayers, I found myself sinking into a shadowy abyss of the ego's making. Instead of seeing light, lifetimes of grievances, unfairness, resentment, sorrow and abandonment oozed from hidden crevices in my mind, swirling, stifling all hope, taking on a force that I could not ignore, a giant whirlpool of blackness engulfing every fibre of my being. Oddly, and also most fortunately, I was able to completely set aside the darkness when it came to working with clients. What I found to be even more odd, was that I found myself experiencing greater insight and clarity than ever before when it came to my clients. Just not for myself, where I remained in the dark. And during the quiet moments, when usually there was peace, I found the darkness to be most intrusive. In fact, in the stillness of my mind, peace had gone and left me stranded, drowning in the bleakness of my belief in my eternally damned unholy nature.

Groping blindly in the desolate darkness of my thoughts in search of guidance, I picked up the big blue book and read. This is a time for faith, Jesus reminds us. *This is a time for faith*, I repeated to myself over and over again. The Holy Spirit has heard my plea, and so He has answered. I tried to take my mind off the gloom by watching television, but nothing appealed to me; and as much as I enjoyed gourmet cooking, I found no comfort in food. It all tasted the same. Even the garden had lost its magic; it was just a bunch of vegetation, albeit a colourful spread of vegetation, beautiful in the eyes of the world, but my worldly eyes saw no beauty; only darkness. I also stopped writing, the one activity that I found the most enriching at all levels of my being. How could I possibly write a book called "Choosing the Miracle" when the miracle continued to elude me.

This is a time for faith.

Have faith in Him Who answered you.

This was the most difficult stretch of the journey I had yet encountered, I realized, as I waded through a sickly pool of painful emotions ranging from hurt to grief, anger and despair, but worst of all, profound guilt.

I must look at the darkness to get to the light.

I looked, but the darkness remained while the stain of sin settled in my mind—an unsettling testament to my failure as a Course student.

I need do nothing.

What was there to do in the face of this overwhelming guilt? I looked at the darkness; staying with it throughout the days, glad for its absence while I was focused on work, grateful for the respite offered in sleep, hoping it would be gone when I awoke. But each morning, it returned.

> You have never given any problem to the Holy Spirit He has not solved for you, nor will you ever do so. You have never tried to solve anything yourself and been successful. Is it not time you brought these facts together and made sense of them? (T-16.II.9:1–3)

Before going to sleep, I asked the Holy Spirit to help me get through this stretch of darkness. As part of my process in working with the Course, I had found that the best time for hearing guidance was early in the morning, just before getting out of bed, in that quiet moment before the thoughts of the day come to intrude on my awareness. Very often this is when I received answers to my prayers of the night before. So it was that one morning I awoke with a glimmer of insight into the situation. I had been looking at the darkness all right, as we are taught to do in the Course, only I had been doing so with the wrong teacher. I had been looking at the darkness and also gotten sucked right into it, with no way out, because I was looking with the ego. Looked at with the wrong mind, it could only appear very real. Trapped in the ego's clever and slippery nightmare of a thought system, there was nothing to see other than darkness, for to choose with the ego is to renounce the light. Light and joy and peace cannot abide in a world made up to hide them. My problem was that I had been trying to find a solution on my own and had not been mindful of my choice of teacher; I was doing my own thing, *yet again*. I had forgotten to look with Jesus. Oops!

> It is your thoughts alone that cause you pain. Nothing external to your mind can hurt or injure you in any way. There is no cause beyond yourself that can reach down and bring

oppression. No one but yourself affects you. There is nothing in the world that has the power to make you ill or sad, or weak or frail. (W-pI.190.5:1–5)

See the Problem as It Is

Wanting nothing more than to haul my ass out of this dark pit of despair, I grabbed hold of Jesus' hand, dusted myself off, and got back in the game. The entire situation was all very strange, and very much out of proportion; I had never before experienced such feelings of antipathy for this person, nor for anyone else, for that matter. Clearly, this was none other than an overly inflated fear-based ego-response. All those months of flirting with the thought of reaching for the peace of God and ultimately returning home were taking their toll on my still ego-identified self. While my preference for peace and my yearning for the Love of God had grown stronger, the ego was growing less assured of its special spot in my mind and was understandably increasingly threatened.

The contrast between how it felt to choose with the wrong mind as opposed to choosing with the right mind was stark; it was an experience I would never, ever forget. In fact, it is an experience that would serve to give me pause whenever I caught myself about to choose with the wrong mind. I was aware that the Holy Spirit could not choose for me; and neither could Jesus. However, they could help me see the cause of my distress: my desire to maintain my illusory state of separation. I saw darkness because I continued to choose with the ego, where light cannot be found. At any time, I could make a different choice, a choice I would make when I was ready. I wanted very much to go to my right mind and see the call for love that was behind both sides of this encounter, but I remained stuck in my wrong mind, clinging to the thought that someone could attack me and cause me to lose my peace, essentially, clinging to the darkness of my own choosing.

The necessary condition for the holy instant does not require that you have no thoughts that are not pure. But it does require that you have none that you would keep. (T-15.IV.9:1–2)

Fortunately, Jesus does not expect us to be unfailing experts in the practice of forgiveness; if we were, we would not need his Course. Gently, without judging us, he shows us how we don't want to forgive and how badly we feel because of this. In the face of my own unwillingness to forgive, I was appalled at my lack of progress on this journey. It was, quite frankly, discouraging. In search of comfort, I opened the big blue book to where I had left off the week before, and as expected, I was given a further glimmer of understanding: Lesson 198: "Only my condemnation injures me." I suppose I might have found help in any number of lessons, which seems to be the way with the Course whose message is simple, and consistent throughout, but this happened to be where I was in my review. I thought deeply about how whenever I feel anything but total, unshakable peace, which was, more often that I care to admit, it must be that I had chosen against peace. The mildest judgment, the most seemingly harmless accusation, the smallest resentment, any desire for specialness, a mere hint of defensiveness—all were condemnations of the love that is due my brothers and myself.

Faltering Faith

Not ready to throw in the towel, I didn't back down. I had come this far in my learning, now was the time to put it to good use, besides which, I wanted very much for this to be a healed relationship. But as the days passed, the dark clouds persisted and I began to feel abandoned. This is what it felt like to believe in separation from God; no words can describe the emptiness and the devastation that come with the thought that there is nothing beyond the darkness. Faith began to falter as I doubted that I would ever make it through; in fact, I feared that I would not make it back to where I had fallen off the long ladder home.

As readers of my two previous books know, I am a big fan of the work of Ken Wapnick. In fact, having clocked in well over 2000 hours of his workshops, I dare say, perhaps closer to 2500, I probably fall somewhere in the range of stalker, slow learner and spiritual simpleton. Yet, for the first time ever, I had been unable to listen to my customary late evening Ken Wapnick workshops. For a moment, I hated him, but just for a moment. Why was this Course so damned difficult! It's okay for a holy person like Ken Wapnick to talk about sin, guilt and fear and the simplicity of looking with the right mind and just letting things go and not judging oneself and laughing at the tiny, mad idea; he just about walks on water! I'll bet he can turn water into wine; hell, I'll bet he walks on wine! The rest of us schleps aren't so holy! The rest of us non-holy sinners have to work so much harder if we are going to be allowed anywhere near the gates of Heaven! I grumbled as I flipped through my MP3 player in search of a comforting topic. I still wasn't ready to give up. "Love: Dark Night Living Flame." I had listened to this workshop at least a dozen times; surely it would offer the guidance I needed.

Ken Wapnick explains that it is possible to be in one's right mind, and still feel the discomfort, or the pain. In fact, I must be in my right mind if I am observing myself in any state, whether comfortable or not. This tiny bit of information was encouraging and, in fact, helped me start to turn the corner on the darkness. Though the darkness remained, I was able to appreciate the returning faith in my new choice of Teacher. I was looking without judgment, therefore not adding to the guilt. If I was looking without judgment, I must be in the decision-making part of my mind. This was the seat of all power; the mind's ability to choose. This is the place the ego desperately wanted to keep hidden from me by coaxing my attention out into the world.

So I looked, and waited, always with Jesus now, without judging myself. Which is when I saw clearly that a part of me that identified with the thought system of the ego had chosen to see conflict, it was clinging to the darkness and it wanted to make the pain of separation real. Anything was fair game when it came to maintaining my separated self. As much as I said that I wanted the peace of God, as much as I said that I wanted to see all my brothers sinless, as much as I said that I wanted to see the light of Christ in all my brothers, I wanted my separated existence more. The truth was that there was a part of me that did not want to release my ancient grievances, because it was by the memory of these grievances that I defined myself.

> The ego's voice is an hallucination. You cannot expect it to say "I am not real." Yet you are not asked to dispel your hallucinations alone. You are merely asked to evaluate them in terms of their results to you. If you do not want them on the basis of loss of peace, they will be removed from your mind for you. (T-8.I.2.2–6)

The Ego's Lies

In an email from my dear friend Susan Dugan, she reminded me that the ego lies… and lies, and lies and lies. Yes, the ego wanted me to believe that I was not equal to the teaching of the Course. It had tried to convince me that I could fix the problem on my own, that I had been abandoned by the Holy Spirit, that I was responsible for my brother's loss of peace and that, by all appearances, I did not have what it took to fix the problem, and we won't even talk about my ridiculously lofty goal of a return to Heaven. It wanted me to fail; better yet, it wanted me to quit. But I wouldn't. I trusted that I would be led through this darkness, hopefully sooner, rather than later.

Do you want to see your brother sinless? Jesus asks us.

Yes! I replied from my right mind.

No! Came the wrong-minded response.

Why couldn't I just let it go? Please, just let it go!

The survival of the guilty self I believed myself to be hinged solely on my belief in a long-held lie that said that if I experienced a loss of peace, it was because my brother did something to me. I needed this perception of the situation if I was to establish and prove my innocence; my brother was guilty of an unfair attack and I was an innocent victim. As long as I clung to this picture of myself, I would need to see grievances, a dark veil that would forever keep away the Love of God I so desperately sought.

This spirituality is way over your head, the dark voice said, mockingly. *You are not, and will never be a holy person. The arrogance! What were you thinking! Holy person? Ramana, Brother Lawrence, sure, but you? Come on! What a foolish notion!*

But how could what God created be anything but holy? I countered courageously. Clearly, the ego was lying again; but then, that is all it is capable of. Lies. The ego lies… and lies, and lies and lies. My prayer that night was loud and clear. Enough, I told Jesus. I would not be held hostage by the dark thoughts of an insane thought system.

> If you knew Who walks beside you on the way that you have chosen, fear would be impossible. You do not know because the journey into darkness has been long and cruel, and you have gone deep into it. A little flicker of your eyelids, closed so long, has not yet been sufficient to give you confidence in yourself, so long despised. (T-18.III.3:2–4)

For my Brothers

When I awoke the next morning, I realized that it was not necessary to experience the pain and the anguish of the darkness, even while looking at it. It was all so silly. The process is really quite simple: either you decide for darkness, or you decide for the light. I had come this far, I wasn't about to succumb to the ego's tricks, no matter how clever or how powerful they seemed. Yet, it concerned me that, given everything I had learned, I still had chosen the wrong mind over the right mind, darkness over light. The days passed, a precarious balance between an increasingly bland darkness and thankfully darkness-free work and business activities. Somehow, I was able to continue to do all those little things that were necessary for survival without too much discomfort and ego-intrusion.

I thought of the book that was not being written, and the emails in my Inbox from readers awaiting this next book. Finally, one night I prayed for help in getting through the darkness, if not for myself, then, let it be for my brothers.

I want to get through this for my brothers who travel with me on this journey. Let's do it, I told Jesus. I'm ready to walk through the darkest night if I have to. I will do it for my brothers. I can do it.

Upon waking, I understood why I had found it so difficult to let go of my grievances: I still clung to the fear of love. In asking for help for myself and my brother, I was reminded that we journey to the light together, all brothers, as one, or not at all. This did not mean that my brother had to become a student of *A Course in Miracles*, rather it meant that, since we were in this together, I needed to relinquish all my grievances in order for my brother to be freed from the darkness. As my brother is freed, so I will be freed. If I choose to cling to my grievances, no matter how seemingly insignificant, the light will remain obscured. In letting go of grievances, I, we, will allow the return of the light of truth. I was inspired to write a letter to my friend, with the help of the Holy Spirit. It was a kind, gentle message, expressing the hope of healing and of love. Several nights later, I dreamed that my friend and I exchanged a big huge hug; there was only love between us.

The Holy Spirit's Good Samaritan

My confidence in my work with the Course having been just about wiped out, I had been unable to return to my writing. Only half-jokingly, I considered applying for a job at the flower shop that had opened nearby a few months earlier. A friend of mine even enquired on my behalf about a job opening in a flower shop in his neighbourhood. It was in the midst of this ego outbreak that I received an email from a Mr. Lin from Taiwan, which turned out to be one of those many times in my life when, by an act of grace, I have been gently steered back on track. Mr. Lin was a retired executive who was now devoting his life to teaching and bringing *A Course in Miracles* to the Orient. He was writing to enquire if I would consider translating my book, *Leaving the Desert*, into Chinese. For reasons that my delicate frame of mind couldn't at the time quite fathom, he seemed to think it would be a most helpful book for students in Taiwan and China where there was a rapidly growing interest in the Course.

We exchanged several emails over the weeks that followed, discussing how we could make this happen. In the process, my confidence in my work slowly returned. Perhaps there was some value to my writing after all. But more than that, Mr. Lin was also a very big fan of the written works of one Dr. Kenneth Wapnick plus he had a most impressive knowledge of the Course. Mr. Lin was a rock sent to help steady my faltering steps during the darkest passage of my journey home. As our friendship blossomed, very slowly, my sense of direction was restored and I was able to return, though somewhat tentatively, to my writing. There was no doubt that the crossing of our paths had been guided by the Holy Spirit.

Chapter 6

THE CLOSING OF THE GAP

Miracles rearrange perception and place all levels in true perspective.... Miracles are examples of right thinking, aligning your perceptions with truth as God created it.... A miracle is a correction introduced into false thinking by me. It acts as a catalyst, breaking up erroneous perception and reorganizing it properly.... Miracles arise from a miraculous state of mind, or a state of miracle-readiness. (T-1.23:1; 36; 37:1–2; 43)

The End of Illusions

OCCASIONALLY, READERS AND CLIENTS will ask if I am familiar with other spiritual paths. Very often they are referring to recently released books, new spiritual approaches, teachers they have seen on the Internet, adaptations and supposed improvements to traditional spiritualities, and even new approaches to, and alternate versions of, *A Course in Miracles*. Most of the time I would reply that no, I was not familiar with the works in question, especially the newer ones. After a life-long search, having found a path that worked for me, I really had no interest in pursuing yet another path. That would be way too much work! Besides, to jump ships midstream would only delay the outcome. Although *A Course in Miracles* does state that it is one path among many thousands, it is unique in that it is designed to go straight to its intended destination, no meandering, no dawdling, no getting lost along the way— or at least, that is its intended purpose when studied with the right

Teacher. This is the approach that appealed to the direct, impatient, driven nature of the main character of my script.

I would make my point by explaining that if I wanted to drive from Montreal to Vancouver, I would probably take the Trans-Canada Highway and head west, the quickest and most efficient route. Then of course I would choose a comfortable vehicle, perhaps equipped with a GPS and whatever else I needed to make the journey straight, easy and, of course, comfortable. If I picked a broken-down jalopy, or some experimental hybrid car, I might not reach my destination as quickly, perhaps I might not even reach it at all.

Alternatively, I could head down to New York and then keep going towards New Orleans, continue south for a visit with my cousins in Mexico City, and all the way down to Buenos Aires to stay with another friend; I could meander up the west coast with a few side trips along the way, visit friends in California, and naturally, I would make a slight detour to check in with my good friend Susan in Colorado. If I posted a message on my social networking page, I have no doubt that there would be enough pit stops on the way to make the journey last twenty-five years. Obviously, the straight route would be quicker. The question to ask is how quickly or, how slowly, do I want to make the journey home?

For me, *A Course in Miracles* was the all-inclusive package complete with road map, directions, and a vehicle in the form of a solid metaphysics that would allow me to comfortably navigate the roadways of my life in a manner that ensured that, with persistence, by staying on this path, I would eventually reach my intended destination. It was comforting to be on a path that allowed for enjoyment of the journey while exerting a minimum amount of effort. Okay, I lied a bit, there's always the challenge of dealing with ego roadblocks, potholes and diversions, but, no matter, the goal is set and there is no doubt of its attainment.

I owned a hardcover copy of the official third edition of *A Course in Miracles*, I was a student of Dr. Kenneth Wapnick, and this was the path I was clinging to, come hell or high water. Naturally, having undertaken this journey with my ever-faithful companion—*you-know-who*—never did it occur to me that perhaps I had made the form of my journey just a tad special. Just a tad. By the same token, I had not noticed that my cross-country voyage had become suspiciously homogenous, with very few changes in scenery. But no matter, I was a devoted, dedicated and determined Course student, in possession of an increasingly solid understanding of the metaphysics of sin, guilt and fear, and its chief architect, the ego, and so, I was quite content with my seeming progress on the journey home.

Which is why when Mr. Lin, for whom I had come to have the utmost respect, asked if I had ever heard of a book called *Graduation: The End of Illusions*, a dialogue between Jesus, also referred to as Raj, and a fellow called Paul Norman Tuttle, I felt the ego bristle a bit. We had a good thing going, ego and I; it brought up obstacles on the journey and, as best I could, I dealt with them. Although it had shown itself to be increasingly wise in the ways it could weasel itself into my thinking, I remained unwavering in my holy intent. It was an excellent partnership and we were on a comfortable journey, so, why rock the boat.

No, I thought, in defence of my very familiar, and very comfortable path. *Never heard of it. I had my teacher and my path, and I felt there was enough on my plate with this classroom.* That was my silent, automatic response. There was so much material about the Course cropping up on the Internet that just the sight of it caused me to recoil in confusion. Besides, more and more, I just wanted a simple experience of the truth. But, because of my high regard for my new friend's knowledge of all things relating to *A Course in Miracles*, I told him I would look it up. Mr. Lin was, after all, a "Wapnickian"; surely he was not about to send me on some wild spiritual goose chase. Though at first ambivalent, in the end, curiosity about this work supposedly channelled from Jesus won out. And so it was that when I looked up the recommended reading on the Internet, I was pleased to find that it was available as a free downloadable file on the website of the Northwest Foundation for *A Course in Miracles*.

The Kingdom of Heaven is the dwelling place of the Son of God, who left not his Father and dwells not apart from Him. Heaven is not a place nor a condition. It is merely an awareness of perfect Oneness, and the knowledge that there is nothing else; nothing outside this Oneness, and nothing else within. (T-18.VI.1:4–6)

I devoured *Graduation* overnight. Although at first it took some getting used to the terminology, being somewhat different from that with which I was accustomed, I soon felt as though I had been parachuted into an advanced *Course in Miracles* class. All the bits and pieces of my learning of the previous years, in fact, of my entire life, fell into place, filling in the gaps of the giant puzzle of truth. God is right here, right now; we are smack dab in the middle of the Kingdom of Heaven; we have never left and so there is not really anywhere to go. We are only imagining that we are in dense, physical forms we call bodies.

The reason that this experience seems so real to us is that we have abandoned true perception in favour of the false perception of the senses, a false perception that can only leave us in a state of limited sight and therefore ignorance. With faulty perception, there is only an illusion of reality, a distorted, limited picture of the truth, and so the truth fades from our awareness. An illusion is a fantasy, an empty wish with no power to change reality. While in our childish collective experiment in separation we may have pushed Heaven out of mind and seemingly out of reach leaving us with only an illusion of a world apart from Heaven, in reality, there *is* only the Kingdom of Heaven.

Huh!

God is right here, right now; we are smack dab in the middle of the Kingdom of Heaven.

I pondered this new awareness for days. I already knew all this, but now I *knew* it. I looked back over my life and saw how distracted I had been by my great search for the truth, pursuing all manner of spiritual teachings, when the truth had been there all along. A lifetime spent believing that God was a universe away, that Heaven was unattainable by the likes of me. Fifty-seven years of believing the lie, and the truth had been there all along. The truth had been right beside me, waiting for me to see it.

God is right here, right now; I am in the middle of the Kingdom of Heaven.

I wanted to kick myself for having been such a fool. All at once, I wanted to cry, to laugh, to rejoice and to cry again, grateful for having been shaken out of a spiritual stupor I seemed to have inadvertently fallen into—well, not so inadvertently, given my travel companion. I had effectively driven myself into a rut, wheels spinning, going nowhere fast. I became aware that I had maintained important gaps in my learning, courtesy of my evil conjoined twin—the ego—ensuring that it would be quite a while before I ever saw the light of day. It was as though I had climbed a giant observation tower along the highway of my journey, and from this new vantage point, I realized that the journey was much shorter than I had believed it to be; it was, in fact, a needless journey, for the Kingdom of Heaven is right here, right now.

> *Beyond this world there is a world I want. I choose to see that world instead of this, for here is nothing that I really want.* (W-pI.129.7:3–4)

It was with this new awareness that I sat down to meditate one Sunday afternoon. God was so close. Heaven was here, now; there was nothing else. We are in the middle of the Kingdom of Heaven. Heavy gray clouds had begun to circle the horizon announcing the coming of severe thunderstorms. Through the window facing my meditation spot on the dining room floor, I could see the sun's rays cutting through the trees in a wedge of clear blue early autumn sky.

God is right here, right now.

Usually, I would close my eyes, quiet my mind, and within seconds, enter the quiet space within. This time however, I held my eyes wide open. I wanted to see God. I wanted to sense God's presence. I wanted to know that God was here, now. Tears came easily now, as a profound sense of relief and great joy washed over me. Branches swayed like arms reaching up to Heaven, and through tear-filled eyes, the rays of sunlight shimmered between the leaves like dew-covered diamonds. As I wept, I knew with absolute certainty that God was here, now.

The Miracle as Corrected Perception

Seek only the experience. Do not let theology delay you. The Course does give us very clear guidance. However, evidently, my experience of God's presence on that Sunday afternoon had not sufficiently convinced me that the journey home was made by turning one's attention inwards, and only inwards. Or, perhaps it had been too threatening for that part of my mind that still clung to the ego's promise of a good time to be had as a separated self. Turning my attention, once more, outwards, I sought out the Northwest Foundation's website for more learning material. To my great delight, I found that there were hundreds of hours of recorded workshops and meetings dating back some twenty-five years. Why settle for a momentary shift in perception when hundreds of hours of additional learning awaited, promising even greater shifts. Why settle for a blissful brush with the truth when there must be an even greater truth just around the corner.

Stop talking about going home. Know that you are home. This is the miracle. Why stop now; I was on a roll! And so I jumped back into my vehicle where my trusted co-pilot sat waiting patiently and resumed my spiritual journey. The ego always knows how to draw us back out into the world, and the pursuit of a spiritual goal is no less a distraction than the pursuit of a material goal. All outward pursuits are equally meaningless; in perfect wholeness, there are no pursuits.

In my characteristically compulsive style, I dove right in, devouring as many hours of workshops as I could during my spare time, while cooking, while doing chores and during my daily walks. As I immersed myself in this new approach, my understanding of the metaphysics of *A Course in Miracles* shifted, so that I could see clearly how I had built for myself a learning structure that was logical, even elegant, but, more importantly, it was *safe*. From the ego's perspective, there had been just enough gaps in my understanding to keep me from making a real shift, the most significant gap being this huge chasm I had built between myself and the Kingdom of Heaven. All of this occurred while I had just begun my review of Part II of the Workbook, and with this new understanding, I was astounded at the extent to which I had completely overlooked what it actually said. The truth had been there all along; I simply had not seen it.

> God is with me. He is my Source of life, the life within, the air I breathe, the food by which I am sustained, the water which renews and cleanses me. He is my home, wherein I live and move; the Spirit which directs my actions, offers me Its Thoughts, and guarantees my safety from all pain. (W-pII.222.1:1–3)

I think this is also the first time I really understood what the Course means when it says that the miracle is a sudden shift in perception. Viewed from above the battleground, as a playground filled with children playing make-believe games, the world lost most of its significance. Its only value is that it reflects back to us what we believe to be true. The miracle corrects faulty perception. The perception of form by the senses is the wrong-minded way of blocking out the light, our true expression as God's children. If there is only Heaven, then this is where the sleeping children must be, and the dream must be in the minds of the sleeping children. Where else could anything possibly be? And what of the self that was observing all this? This must be the Self that God created. This sleeping self doesn't just disappear; instead, the waking Self arises to take its place and fulfills its function as God's expression.

With this sudden influx of new insight, I began to feel uncomfortable with the idea of continuing to host my *Course in Miracles* study group meetings. I had come to the conclusion that I didn't know shit. More importantly, I felt uncomfortable with the two books I had so eagerly and sincerely written on the subject: *Making Peace with God* and *Leaving the Desert*. I had been so naive! My understanding had been lacking, even faulty; I had incorrectly learned and represented this teaching. Then there was the small matter of my new book, more than two-thirds finished. It seemed inaccurate now. How could I finish a book that was so steeped in the illusion now that I had seen beyond the illusion! The only solution was to stop writing.

In the midst of this perceptual metamorphosis, my friend Lisa and I got together for lunch. Although we had not scheduled a reading, feeling in dire need of guidance, I asked if she wouldn't mind checking in with our favourite teacher. I needed help. Despite my initial uncertainty about channelled works in general, because of the remarkable accuracy and relevance of her readings, I had grown to respect Lisa's tremendous gift. I was profoundly grateful for the crossing of our paths, something I came to see as an intervention on the part of the Holy Spirit.

Sitting across my desk in the silence of my office, Lisa closed her eyes and, in the quiet, took the time to connect. Eager for the guidance that was forthcoming, I placed a pencil and pad nearby and quieted my mind as best I could. After a couple of minutes, she began. I jotted notes as she spoke, careful to catch the words that sometimes came in short, quick spurts, filtered by Lisa's personal style. While mostly, she allowed Jesus to speak through her, on occasion, she spoke for him, as though he had given her instructions on what to say.

"You are presently in another passage; a dark night of the solar plexus. The soul can't resist doing the clearing, the cleansing; this is needed to share with the world. There is nothing to fear although you do feel fear. Emotions tell us where we are; do not fear the emotions."

Lisa paused, turning her head as though to listen more clearly. "He is showing an image of you lying down with him putting his hand on you at the solar plexus level. Feel him in the emotion, but not in the pain. You need to feel the emotions in order to work with others. Meditate with him and allow his presence at the level of the solar plexus. Simply walk through the passage."

"Stop following and listening to other teachers; just listen to me."

Lisa's message from Jesus was firm, and clear. "I don't want you to continue in that direction. You must have your own power centre with *me*. Prior tools allowed you to connect; now, teachers distract you and put you in your mind only."

"The solar plexus is where a space, a separation remains. It is hard for a human being to understand love from the solar plexus. Allow the healing to occur with me and you will feel more love more joy and more sharing. Walk through the emotions. Whether close to spirit or far from spirit, you feel me everywhere but at the level of the plexus. You need to allow yourself to *feel*. Remember what it is like to have been touched by God. Be touched every day without suffering."

"Separation is an illusion."

"Oneness has no words."

Still excited with the discovery of the Raj material, I was a little disappointed to hear that I should stop my studies. I had really enjoyed those workshops and there was so much more for me to learn. "Do I have to stop listening to Raj?" I asked during a momentary break in the reading.

"No." The answer came quickly, and I was relieved.

"You don't need to be told what to do. Listen to understand more from others who are doing what you are doing."

"Now you have to have a relationship with *me*; our exchanges will have beginnings and endings and conversations."

During another pause in the reading, I enquired about my writing, now at a dead stop. This was a big concern for me and I wanted to know whether or not I was meant to continue with my book—or any books, for that matter.

"You have to *feel* now. You are going somewhere new. If you can't feel it, you can't allow it and you can't write it. You need to feel. Then you can share all this knowledge in your own way, in your own words."

"You will continue."

In my experience with these channelled messages, I had found that they were not always completely clear, at least not right away. Sometimes, parts of a message would only make sense several months later. This time was no different, and so I decided to just let it settle. The parts that were unclear to me were the references to feeling and to the solar plexus; I thought I had felt plenty of emotions over the past months, and I wasn't looking forward to feeling any more than I needed to. I also was not sure about the significance of the solar plexus; it did not seem to relate to my current situation.

What was very clear however was the extent to which I had been relying on the ego as my travel companion. Although I frequently referred to Jesus as my teacher, I had not fully embraced this relationship. We had not had real, two-way conversations, my excuse being that I was not a channeller like Lisa. But now, I made the commitment to strengthen this relationship.

The Master Trickster Out-tricked

Despite that I had been advised to stop following other teachers, having received the green light to continue listening to Raj lectures, I happily got back on the bandwagon and returned to my studies. Unfortunately—yet again, evidence that old habits die hard—I forgot to leave my familiar travel partner behind. While many gaps in my learning were being corrected during my crash course in all things Raj, I began to find myself growing increasingly confused.

There was a marked difference between the approach used by Raj and that used by Ken Wapnick, and the more I tried to reconcile the two, the more muddled I became. I searched the Internet for yet more input, and grew even more confused; there were so many different teachings out there, and no two of them could be fully reconciled. Then I returned to the big blue book itself. Of course, there were more than one versions of it. More confusion.

For the sake of simplicity, I decided to stick with the version of the Course that had crossed my path at the start of my journey. Besides which, I had no scholarly or intellectual interest in validating one version over another. In Part II of the Workbook for Students, we are invited to forget about words and, instead, seek a direct experience of the truth. Since in my new understanding the distance between the world and Heaven had collapsed to nothing, these lessons now had an entirely new meaning. We are in the middle of the Kingdom of Heaven. God is not just a lofty intellectual concept; God is real; God is here, now. This is a concept that needed to be further explored.

> There is no time, no place, no state where God is absent.... I was mistaken when I thought I lived apart from God, a separate entity that moved in isolation, unattached, and housed within a body. (T-29.I.1:1; W-pII.223.1:1)

I had spent the better part of the previous six years studying, analyzing and becoming very well acquainted with the wrong-minded thought system of separation, when in truth, there is only God. I returned to the early Workbook lessons which clearly address the fact that the problem does not lie in the world; rather it resides in our distorted sense of perception and our clinging to a belief that these perceptions are true. The purpose of the Workbook is to clear the mind for an experience of the truth. I quickly scanned several chapters of the Text; again, the invitation to seek the presence of God was woven throughout the theory. What once had seemed lofty and impossible, was now close, very real and made sense; what before had made sense, was logical, tangible and believable had now ceased to be real. Heaven was real; the world was not.

You have to feel now, Lisa had said in that last reading. But who was the "me" that had sensed the presence of God through the window that Sunday afternoon? There was the illusion of a world, and there was the reality of God and the Kingdom of Heaven, and there was "me" in the middle of it all. Everything I had studied and learned crumbled like a house of cards. I had been carjacked and left without a vehicle for my journey. Besides, where was there to go? Up until then, I had assumed the task of navigator of my own journey, and now I came to the full realization that I could go no further on my own. It was the end of the road. That's it; I give up! This is way over my head, Jesus. I really need help.

I wandered about in this death-like existential void for days, until finally, on Thanksgiving morning I awoke with a wholly clear perspective on what had happened, and in particular, on my own journey with this wonderful spiritual teaching called *A Course in Miracles*. Though daunting and perhaps overly sophisticated for the average reader, present company included, the Course has something for every seeker of the truth. However, it is particularly well-suited for logical, intellectual, analytical minds such as mine. While happily studying, learning and embracing this brilliantly logical thought system, the mind is being purposefully kept busy so that it remains unaware of a subtle, but very powerful process of undoing that is occurring at its very foundation. Like a smitten puppy, entranced by the eloquent language and the almost hypnotically consistent and unwavering logic, the unsuspecting, independent, seemingly separated mind is quietly led to its own dissolution, layer by layer, one faulty belief after another. With continued study, it is inevitable that the mind will be completely undone. For those who have asked for a different way of seeing, the outcome is certain, for God would not keep from us that which is our birthright—the wholeness of mind.

The brilliance of the Course lies in its use of the ego-identified mind's arrogance to lead it to its own undoing. The truth is that the sleeping mind has no idea of what is being done to it. In fact, if its students, still functioning from their identification as separated, individual minds, were even mildly aware of what was really being done, they would be able to find countless ways of circumventing the process. If this were possible, then awakening with the help of the Course would be impossible. It is as though the mind were trapped in a cage that was filled to the brim with the clutter of false beliefs about ourselves: a stifling hoard of lies about our inadequacies, failure to meet the needs of others, unmet expectations, disappointments, shortcomings, countless errors, a foolhardy sense of autonomy and independence and the even more foolhardy independent will to continue mindlessly in the same manner, in short, a lifetime of lies generously heaped upon us by the ego.

Unaware of what is really happening, the mind is blindly being undone. Chapter by chapter, lesson by lesson, the mind's overly cluttered cage is being shaken until all the lies and false beliefs begin to break free and fall out. Inevitably, with continued study and application, the student reaches a point of crisis; they can no longer trust the mind that has guided them for a lifetime, the mind that has guided them outwards, and away from the truth. The cage of foolish separateness that had for too long kept the mind safe from the truth finally breaks. There is only one direction in which to turn; toward the inner guidance of the Holy Spirit.

The following morning, I awoke and heard these words very clearly in my mind: *Congratulations! You passed!*

Huh!

Instantly, I realized that, as messy as the process had appeared, it had been powerful and effective in its job of undoing my wrong-minded belief structures. I pondered this new understanding with great joy. My efforts had been guided and purposeful. Jesus had out-tricked the master trickster—the ego. The Course is not designed to lead its students to spew out beautiful, logical statements about either the truth or the illusion. It is designed to undo the mind so that it no longer stands in the way of an experience of the truth. When there are no more thoughts, there is only being, as God created us. Tremendous relief came over me when I realized that I had not wasted my time. This was the beginning of a wholly different dream, the building of a new relationship with the Father, something which could not have occurred had my mind not been wrenched free of the ego's clutches.

Walking with God

It had been a few weeks since my glimpse of the presence of God through my dining room window, and I began to wonder if this had been an accidental occurrence, a once in a lifetime event. My meditations had grown extremely peaceful, even blissful, but I knew that eventually, the experience of peace and closeness to God would have to extend to all moments of the day and be shared with all encounters with my brothers and sisters.

While preparing for my daily walk, as usual, I reached for my MP3 player. This time though, I felt a very clear and strong impulse to leave it on the desk. At first I hesitated, not sure that this was a good idea. For years, it had been my custom to listen to *Course in Miracles* lectures while on my daily walks. This would make for a very quiet walk. However, the message was clear.

Walk in silence today.

Walk with God today.

And so I did, and as I walked through my quiet residential neighbourhood and turned onto the main boulevard, I contemplated this thought: God is here, now. What would it be like to know this, to feel this truth? I felt tremendous peace as I wondered what it would be like to know God's presence, right here, right now. While traffic flowed north and south on the busy boulevard, and brothers and sisters scurried about their important business, I sensed the movement of God's Creation all around us, an all-enveloping love and sense of safety, endless beauty, all flowing through us, around us, in us. As I stood in awe and overwhelming joy at the intersection, waiting for my crossing signal, there was no doubt in my mind that God was right here, right now. I let the tears flow behind my sunglasses. God is here, now.

Instead of words, we need but feel His Love. Instead of prayers, we need but call His Name…."Who walks with me?" This question should be asked a thousand times a day, till certainty has ended doubting and established peace. Today let doubting cease. God speaks for you in answering your question with these words:

I walk with God in perfect holiness. I light the world, I light my mind and all the minds which God created one with me. (W-pII.in.10:3–4 ; W-pI.156.8)

Chapter 7

THE LESSONS OF THE BODY

It is still true that the body has no function of itself, because it is not an end. The ego, however, establishes it as an end because, as such, its true function is obscured. This is the purpose of everything the ego does. Its sole aim is to lose sight of the function of everything. A sick body does not make any sense. It could not make sense because sickness is not what the body is for. Sickness is meaningful only if the two basic premises on which the ego's interpretation of the body rests are true; that the body is for attack, and that you are a body. Without these premises sickness is inconceivable. (T-8.VIII.5)

MEANWHILE, BACK IN THE body, besides the ongoing aches and pains in my shoulders, arms and back, I had contracted an infection in my upper gum. Though growing a bit discouraged, I was not surprised to be encountering these issues with my body. Throughout my life, I had always favoured intellectual over physical pursuits and had oftentimes felt very limited as a body, even resentful of having been born in a physical form. As such, I had also sensed that the body would be among my greatest classrooms. Feeling resentment for the body is a form of attack; this matter would need to be resolved before I could experience my Self as spirit.

A friend of mine had just completed training in Tui Na, a form of traditional Chinese massage, and naturally, I was only too eager to volunteer my aching bones for her to complete her practice sessions.

It was during one of these massages, which were absolutely wonderful, that I received a hint of the help that would be made available on my journey. Lying on the massage table with my face in the "donut hole," I relaxed completely, while Johanne applied gentle manipulations and pressures along the meridians sending waves of warmth and gentle release throughout my body. My thoughts were on nothing in particular, but I was still revelling in my discovery of the closeness of God. When she reached my shoulders, I clearly heard these words: *You will never again be alone,* which caused me to release a torrent of tears into the donut hole. I knew that Jesus would always be with me, and I felt overwhelmed with relief, knowing that I did not have to journey alone.

Though the Tui Na massages did offer much relief, within days, the various pains invariably returned. Given my profound aversion to traditional medicine, I needed a natural solution, fast. In my meditations, I asked Jesus to help me understand this situation and what I might do to resolve it. After accepting Jesus' invitation to engage in open conversations with him, I had followed an urge to acquire a digital recording device. The model I wanted just happened to be on sale at half price the day I went into the store to make my purchase. I brought the recorder with me when I meditated, and also kept it on the dresser next to my bed at night to catch those early morning messages.

The following insights came to me over the span of a couple of days, some during meditation, and some upon waking in the morning. I was surprised at the extent of the information coming into my mind, and was very glad to have picked up that recorder. Other than a few minor edits for readability, what follows is pretty much how it came:

"In perceiving yourself as a physical, dense body, you are holding on to the illusion that separation is possible. It is an entirely unnatural experience, and must therefore ultimately lead to feelings of discomfort. In order for your body to be healed, the battle in which you have engaged in for most of your life, this false perception of yourself must be healed.

"Perception of bodies, and all form, for that matter, is an attempt to capture the flow of creation and make it one's own. It is an attempt to densify, and imprison spirit. Being that nothing can live outside of God, matter can therefore never represent real life. The body attempts to hold life against infinity in what appears like time. It is not the body that needs healing, it is the relinquishment of the desire to have an experience that is independent from the Father that is needed. This is what is unnatural. This is what must inevitably cause pain and discomfort on some level.

"In your case, since you have much intellectual understanding, the resistance must fall, or be expressed somewhere, and so it falls in the part that you value least spiritually but still value individually: the body. It is your fear of losing your individuality that causes you to cling to your perception of yourself in this densified form. Once you begin to experience the fullness of yourself as spirit, as light, the densified form will no longer be a disturbance or a distraction. In fact, it will no longer feel dense. It will feel light, like spirit. It will be incapable of disease or discomfort.

"You continue to cling to your perception of yourself as a physical body because you believe you still have need of the body as an object for conveniently projecting guilt onto. It is your belief in guilt that causes you to cling to this perception of yourself. At this point, you continue to hold onto the belief that you are not worthy of that next step of going completely into the state of enlightenment to which you are entitled. You still believe that you are not worthy of the Kingdom of Heaven. However, you have now reached a state where you have learned enough to understand, at least intellectually, that you must already *be* in the Kingdom of Heaven because nothing else exists.

"So now you feel as though you are trapped between two beliefs. One that is true and one that is false. The only way out of this dilemma is to move forward. The thought that says that you are guilty and not worthy of the Kingdom is a habit. You need to move forward now with a new habit. Miracles are habits. The shift in perception is a habit. Choose the shift in perception. Over and over again. A thousand times if needed. Practise the miracle. Practise choosing the miracle. Practise choosing to see the truth about yourself. Say "no" to the lie. Simply disregard it. Practise choosing the miracle.

"You have studied enough and you have enough learning now to know what is going on and how to recognize that this world is an illusion. This should give you sufficient motivation to practise choosing the miracle. The learning is complete. By choosing the miracle, you put yourself in a frame of mind and readiness to experience awakening. You still have difficulty believing that it is possible for you to awaken. You still believe in your unworthiness.

"Practise choosing the miracle so that you can believe in your worthiness, as God created you, as God knows you to be right here right now in the Kingdom of Heaven. This is the practice. Looking was the first step, and looking was necessary in order for you to see the difference between the outcome of choosing with the ego as compared to choosing with your right mind, the Holy Spirit. Now you have a basis for comparison. Now you know, by experience, what it feels like to choose with the ego versus what it feels like to choose with the Holy Spirit. They do lead to two completely different experiences. To choose with the ego leads to experiencing guilt, unfulfillment, uncertainty, doubt, conflict; to choose with the Holy Spirit leads to an experience of peace, moments of indescribable wholeness and joy, as when you walked down the boulevard and knew that God was everywhere, right here right now.

"When you choose with the wrong mind you know there's something wrong; you feel lost, isolated, alone, you feel guilty for not having made it home. You feel incomplete and cold. You feel pain in the body. When you have chosen with the right mind, when you have chosen to see from that place in the mind that is whole, you feel peace. Warmth. Safety. This is again a time for faith. This is again a time to abandon the isolation. This is not a journey you can do alone. Take my hand. Come. We go together now.

"As we get closer to the end of the journey, the ego will use whatever means at its disposal to attract your attention. It will use the journey, it will use your writing, it will use your intention to go home—it will use everything that you believe to be important—it will use these things to frighten you, to add guilt, to insert doubt. Do not give the ego anything it can use. Let go of the thinking and the studying and the learning. Let go of everything now and allow the process of healing to occur. There is no need to analyze; there is no need to reason; there is no need for logic anymore. It is finished. There is only the need to allow God to *be* through you. There is no more senseless journey.

"You don't need to plan or justify and try to figure out what to do next. What needs to be done will arise in its own time. You don't have to ask for what to do every minute of the day. Again, just do what needs to be done normally. What you don't need to do, or what you need to give up, is worrying and fussing and analyzing and trying to understand and make sense of a world that is clearly insane. This life can be much simpler and much more fulfilling when you give up being the boss of your life. Give it up now.

"This is what the words mean: I need do nothing. It doesn't mean I need do nothing in the world, it means I need do nothing to make perfection happen. It means I need do nothing of my own independent, separate will. What you need do is less planning, thinking, controlling, analyzing, organizing, all of which just gets in the way of the natural flow of God's expression. Trust that you are the best vessel you can be to allow the expression of God's Light, Love and Wisdom. Let go. Let go. Let go of your hold on what you call your life. Place it all in the hands of the Father. Disease, pain, discomfort all come from holding on to what is not natural. Let go of your hold on the unnatural; allow the natural expression of God to be."

No doubt in reaction to my rapidly growing understanding of the mechanics of healing, I awoke in the middle of night with a migraine, for which I took a couple of ibuprofen. Half my face and neck throbbed in pain from the infection in my gum. As I lay in bed I thought again of this body with which I appeared to be doing constant battle. If I had a spouse or if I still had children in the house, the battle would probably be directed towards them. Since I was alone, it needed to be projected onto something or someone outside my mind, the body being the most likely target.

I became aware of how, even in my quiet, resting state, in the warmth and comfort of my own bed, my body was tense. My hands were clasped into tense fists. This was a surprising revelation, since I believed myself to be a relatively peaceful and relaxed person. Even my shoulders were scrunched up as I lay resting on my side. It was as if the false self was using every ounce of its will to squeeze my being into a highly unnatural dense form. Squeeze, squeeze, squeeze. There was tremendous effort expended in the application of will for the spirit to be what it is not, a physical body. This process of densification was an ongoing choice which I continued to make in my mind. When I awoke in the morning, further instruction awaited my attention; fumbling on the dresser for my glasses, I grabbed the recorder and pressed "record."

"While in meditation, imagine releasing every fibre of tension from your being. Allow more of yourself to be spirit, as God created you. Remember to do this as many times as you can throughout the day. Spirit cannot be held captive in a dense form. Shift your awareness from this imagined dense form to the light that is your real form."

As a means of obtaining relief from the tension in my back, I had taken to meditating while in a modified shavasana pose, lying on my back with my calves elevated and resting on a footstool. This seemed to provide temporary relief, something I would do a few times a day. Towards the end of one of these resting meditations, I was inspired to prepare some Bach Flower Remedies for the infection in my gum. This approach had worked for me before. But I hesitated, judging this to be a desperate measure because, according to the Course, it was in the realm of magic. What I really wanted was true healing, which is of the mind. Once again, I asked for help of my teacher.

"Don't be a hero! Though a form of magic, you should not dismiss the Bach Flower Remedies, or any form of medicine that might be helpful, for that matter. Use the Bach Flower Remedies because you have studied them and you know that they work. The reason they work so well for you is that they are closer to the source of the problem then denser forms of remedies like pharmaceuticals or vitamins and mineral supplements. The Bach Flower Remedies work at the level of thought and feeling. They do not work at the level of illness. In this way, they are oftentimes very effective.

"Once your mind is returned to wholeness, you will be able to heal, as you did when you healed your daughters. Anyone whose mind is healed can heal, if this suits the purpose. When you held your daughter in your arms against your chest, there was nothing but love. There was no fear, no worry, no doubt, no uncertainty, because where there is love nothing can intrude. This is why instantaneous healing was possible in that case. This will be possible again when your mind is fully healed.

"To neglect or mistreat the body in any way, whether it be through improper diet, excessive eating, or the consumption of unhealthy substances, is to attack that which you are now making, a dense model of your spirit self. It is an act of self-hatred. Forgive yourself for having believed that limiting your awareness of your self in a dense form could somehow offer you safe haven from the imagined wrath of an imagined vengeful god. It is all very silly, and can only arise in a moment of insanity. In your growing wisdom, you can now detect those thoughts and impulses that come from insanity, and quietly say no, replacing them with more sane thoughts.

"Do not look down at, demean, mistreat, disrespect or ignore the body. Instead, embrace it for its potential for helping you experience the truth. Look at it, through it, the same way that you would look at the ego. You look at it and smile. And in the same way, look at and smile at the body because, how can an illusion, a simple misrepresentation, block the truth of spirit unless you choose to allow it to do so? Do not hate the body. It is only a limitation if you accept that this is all that you are. Look at it without hatred, fear, frustration or resentment. It is true that it is not real, that it is a misperception of what you truly are. But that is not yet your belief because you still trust the information obtained from your physical senses. Respect where you are now in your beliefs about yourself and your body.

"In your desire to experience yourself as spirit, you are attempting to get rid of the body through the senses. You are seeking to have an experience that is beyond the body by utilizing the means of the body. The experience comes from mind not from thoughts, wishes or desire. The experience comes from spirit. Be curious to know yourself as spirit. Ask to know yourself as spirit. Where is spirit? Where is the light? Where is the truth? The body is nothing by itself. Do not be afraid of it. Do not be afraid of its seeming limitations. It is a foolish device. Smile at it. It is designed by an insane mind. Smile at it, but do not demean it. Do not demean it because you temporarily believe in its worth, and its value. By demeaning the body you are demeaning your ability to choose. You are attacking yourself. You are demeaning your mind. The body is nothing more than a misperception of yourself. You cling to it so hard, to the exclusion of your real self; you no longer experience your real self as spirit.

"Love yourself, for you are the Child of God, worthy of His Love, therefore worthy of yours. To deny this love is to deny what God is: Love. Love your body so that it can serve you well on your journey home. When your mind is joined with God's, there can only be love and a loving intent. Be assured that you are not on the ego's schedule; you are not at the ego's mercy. It remains always your choice to heal, right now."

Don't be a hero.

94

Okay. That was loud and clear. How true, and also very practical. Once again, I felt relieved. I mixed up some Bach Flower Remedies for the aches and pains, using those flowers that were appropriate for my frame of mind, including Crab Apple to cleanse my system of the infection. Within days, much of the muscle pain subsided, as did the infection. My mind was on a guaranteed journey to wholeness; the body would eventually have to follow.

But I still had a couple of concerns regarding the body, and so I posed them to my teacher.

"To think of myself as just thought, or spirit, feels a bit cold. It's like there is nothing left anymore."

"And you think the body is hot?"

I burst out laughing. My teacher did have a wonderful sense of humour, thankfully, since I tended to take things far too seriously.

I also wanted to understand how, if all we are capable of in our separated state is to imagine, and imagination has no real power, how could it be helpful to imagine myself releasing the tension in my body?

"You imagined yourself as a body, a false expression of yourself; you can just as easily imagine yourself as spirit, which is your true expression. Work with what you have."

Okay. I get that. I can work with that. Always the practical teacher. Thank you.

Chapter 8

NEW PURPOSE FOR AN ANCIENT JOURNEY

Learning is useless in the Presence of your Creator, Whose acknowledgment of you and yours of Him so far transcend all learning that everything you learned is meaningless, replaced forever by the knowledge of love and its one meaning. (T-18. IX.12:6)

*G*IVEN MY ALTERED PERCEPTION of all things Heaven and earth, I needed a little time out to dust myself off and regain my bearings. I needed to find, once again, another new normal. The past and the future seemed to merge into the present moment, separate parts of one whole. As quickly as questions arose, clarification came to mind. One issue after another was addressed with equal clarity. When I wondered why I had not received such guidance earlier in my life, why I had been left alone to search a lifetime for the truth that had been there all along, I was shown a long series of events, all of which had clearly been marked by the hand of Divine Guidance.

As for questions I had often posed when I was young: why had I been born a girl? Why had I not been born a boy in Tibet or in India, where I felt I would have been more at home? Or questions about my career inclinations: Why had I simply not followed in my father's footsteps and become an engineer where I would have been assured material security and no doubt a much more straightforward existence? No matter the topic, answers were equally forthcoming. In this new light, I understood that my life had been just right, in that it had served its purpose. No matter how incongruous or illogical my life choices and circumstances might have appeared, they now came together as a united script with the purpose of serving my brothers and my sisters on the journey.

If I had been born elsewhere, given my monk-like nature, I might have headed straight for a cave in Tibet, in which case, my life would have served a very different purpose, as it would have had I become an engineer, or chosen anything but the path I had followed. At the same time, as much as I valued my quiet time for meditation and walking with God, I also understood that to isolate myself now would not serve the greater good and that I could be in the presence of God anytime, anyplace. The real monastery is in my mind.

After starting to work with *A Course in Miracles*, I began to question the purpose of my work with astrology and numerology. These bodies of knowledge remained in the realm of time, and therefore were in the domain of the ego. Just as I had recently come to respect the body for its teaching and learning potential, I came to respect these ancient sciences as tools that I could turn over to the Holy Spirit. It really does not matter what we do in the world as a job; the question remains always: with whom are you doing it?

I realized that the work I was doing was very helpful, even though I was using tools from the dream. I was working with my brothers and sisters who were dreaming, and yes, I was helping them to have more comfortable dreams, but there was nothing wrong with that. Anything that helped a person live better and become more self-aware should never be demeaned. Because one was dreaming it did not mean that one had to suffer. In fact, to be experiencing a happy dream would make the journey home much more comfortable. I was coming to the conclusion that I should not alter my career path when, upon waking one morning, I heard very clear guidance on this question.

"You are not going to work in a flower shop!"

Although I had not been completely serious about making this career move, nor had I thought about it in a while, I found the message amusing. When I went for my afternoon walk that day, I was even more amused, and perhaps even slightly amazed to see a large, hand-written sign on the door of the flower shop of my imaginings: *Store Closing*.

Huh!

Within days of having mixed a batch of Bach Flower Remedies for my various health issues, the pain in my body began to subside; the infection in my gum disappeared within a week. Not long after, I began to get the strong hunch that I should consult an osteopath. The ones I knew had very long waiting lists, so I put in a call with two new osteos. In less than a week, I had an appointment with a practitioner who specialized in posturology, and though I didn't know quite what this approach was, it seemed to be what I needed. I also continued to "imagine" myself releasing the tension from my body during meditation, and as often as I remembered during the day. Over the weeks that followed, the pain in my back continued to subside. Once again focussing on work, I found more joy, and experienced even greater insights when working with clients.

The End of Senseless Seeking

It was an autumn weekend, and I was working in the garden, cutting back branches and gathering up fallen leaves. I had decided not to bring my MP3 player this time, having grown increasingly fond of the quiet. It was cloudy, but not cold yet. As I filled the bags with garden waste for recycling, I found myself thinking about my writing and my work with the Course. I thought about the many spiritualities available in the world today and the many different ways of practising the Course, when I felt a surge of guilt and anxiety. I had been following up some links on the Internet about the Course and once again, became confused. One of my fears was that I would not for a very long time feel what I had felt on that beautiful sunny afternoon while walking in the presence of God. I knew it was one of those passing moments of grace; yet, I wanted to be close to God again.

One thing became suddenly very clear: I did not want to go down that road of confusion ever again. *Enough!* I was tired of seeking. I tied up the third and final bag for the green recycling, and brought it to the side of the house. *No more!* I'd had enough. Climbing the ladder home was like a never-ending climb up a downward escalator. I wanted no more of it. *Enough, enough, enough!* I said, to myself, the ego, to Jesus and to whomever else might be eavesdropping.

"Then stop. End the seeking right now. There is no more need of it. You know enough."

The words came from that now familiar gentle guidance that is never far from my awareness.

Absolutely! There was no more need of endless studying and learning and trying to understand a myriad new approaches when the goal was clear, and simple. There was no more need to climb. It was time to just *be*. I gathered my gardening tools, closed up the shed and decided to go for a long walk. This time, as I debated whether or not to bring my Walkman, I felt the urge to delete all the Course-related lectures from the device and replace them with meditation music.

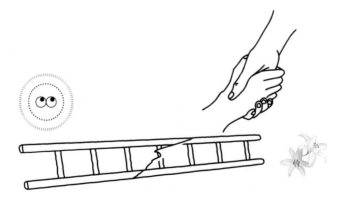

As I walked, surrounded by the soothing strains of the music in my MP3 player, a profound calm came over me. My entire being was peaceful. I knew that I no longer needed to fill my head with all sorts of clutter and noise. I cherished and valued the quiet more than the noise of learning. In the quiet state, I could recall the nearness of the presence of God. When there was noise it was very far away. It was a distance I no longer wanted to experience.

There were a lot of cars on the road for a Sunday afternoon; and as I watched my brothers and sisters drive about in their dream lives I simply loved them. Each one I encountered in the grocery store exuded great beauty. It was a pleasure to walk through the playground with my brothers and sisters knowing that God was nearby. I was relieved that I no longer needed to climb the ladder home. Home was right here. God is right here; the Kingdom of Heaven is right here, right now. All one needs is to step aside from the noise and allow the truth to reveal itself.

> Leave all illusions behind, and reach beyond all attempts of the ego to hold you back. I go before you because I am beyond the ego. Reach, therefore, for my hand because you want to transcend the ego. My strength will never be wanting, and if you choose to share it you will do so. I give it willingly and gladly, because I need you as much as you need me. (T-8.V.6:6–10)

Keep Moving Forward

While life was returning to normal, I still had not returned to writing. Though I sensed that I would finish this book, I was clueless as to how to approach it. Jesus, through Lisa, had clearly conveyed that I was to continue to write, and that my purpose was to share, but I didn't see how. What I had written now seemed obsolete. Once again, as I awoke one morning, I was given very clear guidance.

"You are going to write the book as it is. That is its purpose. It will be most helpful for others to witness the shift from one level of understanding to the next. I will help you. Just keep moving forward."

Okay, I told Jesus. Let's do it. And back to the beginning of the manuscript we went.

Keep moving forward.

I guess Jesus was being nice, not wanting to discourage me too much, when he said that I would write the book "as is." Although it turned out that much of the original material was relevant and remained in the final version, in the end, most of the chapters needed reshuffling, which meant a couple more rounds of edits and patching up.

Though I did not really want to go back in time and study the chakras, a subject I had studied decades ago but did not feel called to pursue at this time, I was curious about what Lisa had said during our last meeting. Given the significant relevance of her readings and my gratitude for the guidance I had been receiving from Jesus, I decided to dust off some old books and see if there might be something helpful for me to apply to my own healing. It didn't take long to find the connection between the solar plexus and trust. I needed to stop thinking, and simply trust. The healing of the solar plexus is the healing of trust. I needed to trust. And listen, which is what I did when guidance, once again, was forthcoming.

"You asked the question, Who is it that wants to know? Who is the self that is watching all this and learning all this? Only spirit is true. Matter is a misinterpretation of what is. It is a substitute for what is. To attempt to understand the truth or spirit with the senses is foolish, it is impossible to understand with the tools that were made to validate matter. Do not seek to know spirit through the senses. This is why you are being asked to feel. Feeling from the solar plexus will allow you to know. Trust comes from the solar plexus. Trust that you will know. If you have asked the question, the answer will come. You cannot receive the answer from the wrong medium, the senses. It must come through experience.

"The analytical mind is designed to process information from the senses; it is not designed to experience spirit. You can only begin to experience spirit through feeling, not through intellect. This is why in many ancient practices a significant part of the training requires quieting of the mind, clearing the way by controlling thoughts. You cannot feel or experience the truth or spirit if you are thinking. Thinking must stop. Thinking gets in the way of the experience. Feeling is closer to being than thinking. Nor can you think your way into feeling. Stop the thinking, as in meditation, and simply allow being to happen. You are right when you say the truth comes to the quiet mind. When the mind is quiet thoughts do not get in the way of the experience.

"Therein also lies the value of mindless, repetitive, what you called monastic tasks, that do not involve extensive thinking and that certainly do not involve analysis. While the senses and the lower mind are busy with something mindless, once again you are in a miracle-ready condition. Simple tasks place you closer to the experience of the truth, or the presence of God, than complex intellectual tasks. This is why whenever you are engaged in these simple tasks, you should have respect for what they really represent."

So it was that in my writing, whenever I hit a roadblock, I made it a conscious point to stop, empty my mind, go for a walk, meditate and wait for inspiration. Whenever the tiniest doubt arose, these words came to take its place: *Keep moving forward.* Without fail, and despite serious attacks of self-doubt, I received the inspiration I needed to bring the manuscript to completion.

> The journey to God is merely the reawakening of the knowledge of where you are always, and what you are forever. It is a journey without distance to a goal that has never changed. Truth can only be experienced. It cannot be described and it cannot be explained. (T-8.VI.9:6–9)

Chapter 9
BEYOND THE ILLUSION

Beyond this world there is a world I want. I choose to see that world instead of this, for here is nothing that I really want. (W-pI.129.7:3–4)

WHEN I WAS LED to understand that I would receive the help I needed to finish this book, I didn't for a moment think that it would be written for me; that was my job. I was only too glad that my skills could be put to good use, and honoured to place them in the service of the Holy Spirit for the benefit of all. Throughout the process of revision, which turned out to be a whole lot more work than I had expected, (A tiny detail that my teacher, turned editor-in-chief, neglected to tell me, no doubt to keep me from bailing out, which I would have done, had I known just how much work there would be!) I frequently reminded myself to just keep moving forward. Very frequently! Corrections needed to be made to the way in which I had presented the metaphysics of the Course, a task that appeared rather daunting, and so every step of the way, I cleared my mind, asked for help, and waited for guidance. Well, that was my intention most of the time, at least when I was able to remember that this wasn't going to be a one-woman job. Actually, it was during those times that I thought I was my own boss that the writing stopped.

Although I had already elaborated on the mythology of the Course in my previous books, this time the thought system of the ego had been very neatly laid out right down to the four splits as taught by Kenneth Wapnick, spiced up with fun illustrations by Alexander Marchand. For years I had been quite comfortable talking about the Son's decision for separation, about how the Son had accepted the ego's invitation to live in a world apart from God, and how all of it was an illusion, sustained by the deeply repressed guilt and fear over a belief in sin. Actually, I think I took a certain perverse pleasure in teaching and talking about the mind-stumping theory of non-dualism with all its savoury separating details. Interestingly, after years of working with the mechanics of separation, there was little, if any, discomfort, anxiety or ego retaliation, a fact that should have raised at least a tiny bit of alarm. *Hello!*

My presentation of the myth of the Course was well-organized and logical, which, though metaphysically correct, remained a presentation of something that was not real, an illusion. I had learned to present the information in such a way that it left out what *was* real: God and the Kingdom of Heaven. All wrapped up in this neat presentation of a false world of its own making, the ego remained safe. This way of looking at the world had been non-threatening to my ego-identified self because it kept God at a very safe distance. Looking back, I realized that it was with a very frightened ego that I had undertaken this bold new journey. It was inevitable that I would organize this unusual spiritual teaching in a way that carried the least amount of threat to what I had for lifetimes believed to be the truth.

Early in 2011, I posted a question on a social media website: What aspect of the teachings of *A Course in Miracles* do you find the most difficult to learn and apply in your life? One might have expected questions about how to be kind and loving in a difficult relationship, or, how to apply forgiveness. Instead, two replies stood out as being very important issues for students: Taking it on faith that this world is not real and, the fact that God is not even aware of this universe of time, space and form. These are indeed big items for students of the Course, issues which I too found difficult to reconcile.

In order to properly address these questions, it was necessary for me to stand very far back, to ask the question from the broadest possible perspective. We might begin with the matter that we have no trouble taking it on faith that this world is real and that there is nothing beyond it that is real. We take it on faith that because we can touch, feel, smell and taste a thing that it is real. We do not question what is this experience of interacting with physical objects. We do not question the messages sent from our sensory apparatus to our brains that interpret the data.

We might ask: if there is a God, why do I not see Him? Why do I not experience Him? If there is a God, and I do not see him, how then can I come to know Him? If the Father is truly loving, He must be aware of us somewhere; perhaps it is that we are not aware of Him! Perhaps it is we who have blocked Him out. We are the ones who have chosen to be separate from Him. We have turned our backs on Him. Perhaps if we were to want to join with Him we would know that He has never stopped loving us.

The truth is that the world is not *just an illusion*; the world we see is a substitute for *something*—a replacement for the truth. What is in front of my face is God; it is my vision that is temporarily out-of-order, so while in the illusion, while seemingly asleep in a dream, I perceive something dark, something dense, something instead of what is really there, spirit. What we suffer from when we believe ourselves to be nothing more than separate bodies, distinct one from the other, with minds that can make decisions that are somehow separate from the one mind, is a collective case of *misperceptionitis*, or, faulty perception.

The Course says clearly that God is in everything; God is everywhere; there is nowhere that God does not exist. The problem is not the world; the problem is with our *perception* of the world. It is how we see the world. We do not see the world as God created it. We see the world as we made it up to be, as dreamers in a dream. If there is

God
The Kingdom
of Heaven

no false world then there must be a real world in its place. The world of form is a made-up way of seeing. It is a substitute for reality that exists only on a limited, perceptual level. The outside world exists only as long as we identify with the projected body. There appears to be a physical world outside the mind only as long as there appears to be an independent perceiver, looking for something or someone outside which can validate the experience of separation. When we abandon our addiction to our separate individuality, the mind is healed, and all relationships are healed. It is how we *see* that is the problem. There is no place where God does not exist. This means that God must be here, now. What God creates must be whole and innocent, which means that if I see my brothers as anything but whole and innocent, I must be seeing incorrectly.

In my eagerness to portray the story of "miscreation," I had forgotten that a myth is just a made-up story, used for illustration purposes. It is not true. When this new perspective first dawned on me, my initial reaction was to berate myself for my foolhardiness. However, having learned that neither the body, nor my work as an astrologer-numerologist should be demeaned, it wasn't a big leap to conclude that neither should my journey with *A Course in Miracles* be demeaned. It is only natural that we would have built-in safety mechanisms when it comes to learning a transformative teaching such as the Course. We cannot learn something that we are not prepared to assimilate. Driven by my almost compulsive desire to experience the truth, I had done my best, learning at the pace that was right for me, and so the learning had unfolded according to my plan of awakening.

Just keep moving forward.

There was still the matter of what to do with this troublesome chapter, and so I asked for guidance, trusting that I would be given the help I needed. Once again, I awoke in the morning with a clear idea of how to handle the material in question: by creating a chapter called "Beyond the Illusion," I would be able to make the necessary adjustments. The first order of business was to remove those sections that neatly illustrated the myth of separation. That approach had served me well at the start of my journey with the Course, but now it had become somewhat of a stumbling block, especially since the ego had learned to circumvent the learning, inserting just enough gaps to keep me from a more complete vision of the truth. It was time for a new road map. For those who share the journey with me, we are now being called to move forward in our learning and for that, we need to let go of our training wheels. It is time to dare to experience our true nature. It is time to be curious about the truth and to cease our dilly-dallying with endless theories and presentations of the illusion. It is time to seek an experience of our true Selves as spirit, as God created us.

If, as the Course makes clear, only God is true and everything else is illusion, this means that our true place is with God, therefore, in the light, meaning enlightened. To desire enlightenment is simply to desire to experience our true state, our birthright as children of God. Any other state is illusory. Jesus reminds us that we are with him, which means that we are like him, already enlightened. The only question that needs be asked is, how long do we want to delay the inevitable remembrance of our true condition? Each one of us has the power to turn from the darkness and look toward the light. That is a fact. To continue to cling to the darkness is to cling to the illusion. To be in the light is as God would want us to be. Enlightenment is therefore not something that we earn for good behaviour; it is God's Will that we experience enlightenment because it is our natural condition. It is ours for the choosing when we decide that the darkness is not a worthy state for a child of light. It is right here, right now.

Answering the Call

Holiness, enlightenment, nirvana, awakening, Samādhi, attainment of the real world—all are variations on what seems like a lofty goal, out of reach for the common mortal, even impossible to attain. Yet, Jesus tells us in the Course, this is our true, natural state, a condition which remains unchanged, the attainment of which actually demands very little effort. It does not require lifetimes of suffering, deprivation and sacrifice, years of prayer, discipline, meditation, celibacy, poverty and fasting, the shaving of one's head or the donning of sandals and ochre robes. Nor does it require initiation into an exclusive cult, walking barefoot across a burning desert, the overcoming of life-threatening obstacles, the maiming of body parts, the signing over of one's inheritance or the achievement of impossible feats. Those are merely distractions, the requirements for making the journey of awakening from the dream more interesting, or perhaps ways of making the dream last just a bit longer. The best kept secret is that the requirement for holiness is really quite simple: that we have no other desire.

> Miracles should inspire gratitude, not awe. You should thank God for what you really are. The children of God are holy and

the miracle honors their holiness, which can be hidden but never lost. (T-1.I.31)

The attainment of our wholeness as God created us asks only that we be willing to look without judgment, that we have the humility to accept responsibility for having chosen against it, and that we be ready to trust in a process that will enable us to undo the lie that keeps us from our inherent holiness. It requires that we be willing to acknowledge that the goals we have so passionately and steadfastly pursued throughout our lives have not brought us the wholeness we truly seek, and most likely never will. More importantly, and this is the seemingly difficult part, it asks that we be willing to examine the fact that we have chosen these unfulfilling goals in a foolish attempt to distract ourselves from our deeply buried fear that we might one day claim our natural wholeness.

What makes the attainment of wholeness seem impossible is that we have lost touch with the true source and cause of all of our experiences here, in bodies, in a seemingly very real world: our decision for separation, our belief in the guilt over that choice, and the need to keep this knowledge far from our awareness. Essentially, what keeps us from our wholeness is our belief in a lie, a lie that feeds our addiction to our seeming experience of separateness from our Father. Since we believe in time, we no longer see that we have the power in our minds to choose for our wholeness now; we think it is something to be aspired to in the future. At least at the beginning of our healing journey, we are completely unaware of this power, oblivious to the fact that every moment of every day we continuously choose either to remember or to forget. Because that place in our mind where we can make a different choice appears completely hidden from our awareness, we need a good teaching that will help us return to our mind. What keeps us from our wholeness is a thought of separation—and thoughts can be changed.

A spirituality such as *A Course in Miracles* tends to draw people who have experienced some form of discomfort or pain, whether physical or emotional, most often the latter, at one time or other in their lives. Its title alone evokes a promise of a benign divine intervention in the affairs of a world that appears to be in dire need of a miracle. To a certain extent, membership in most, if not all religions and sects, is built and sustained by appealing to the pain and suffering of the masses. A promise of peace and especially the hope of forgiveness from God can have a very strong power of attraction for the broken, the lost and the disenfranchised soul. The challenge is to find a path that delivers on its promise.

The Course is for whomever hears its call, and people of all ages, races, creeds, cultures and walks of life have embraced its powerful healing message. Though there are certainly some, perhaps even many such individuals, I have yet to meet anyone who was living a perfectly charmed, happy life who picked up the big blue book and decided to read it for the sheer enjoyment of its sophisticated writing style—not to mention the thrill of examining their deeply repressed sin, guilt and fear and the insanity of projection as our chosen solution to a problem we made up in the first place—and instantly embraced its mind-bending metaphysics. Because of our deep fear and resistance to relinquishing the idea of a separated self, the journey home is bound to lead its students through a few bumpy patches before the true joy of our return to the truth is uncovered.

Many people are first attracted to the Course after having spent years in search of the truth, tired of the same old unsatisfactory answers to questions about the origins of life and the meaning of existence. From an early age, they experienced a vague, or some-times even very clear impression that things in this vast universe simply did not add up. This divine discontent is what prodded them to continue searching. There is usually an accompanying feeling of readiness when they begin to read the Course: This is what I have been looking for all my life! Deep down, they know that the Course came into their life at the right time, almost as though it were an appointed time. This recognition is often accompanied by a sense that this is a key turning point in a lifelong quest and that life is about to take on a whole new direction and, quite frequently, it does.

Others come to the Course in desperate need of answers and help, usually when situations in their lives have become intolerable. They have likely tried to solve their problems by delving sincerely into numerous self-help, New Thought, New Age or spiritual teachings and practices. Having experienced limited, or even a complete lack of success with these approaches, still in need of relief from pain, sorrow and grief, typically drained, discouraged and disillusioned, they turn to *A Course in Miracles*, often recommended by a friend. "Here," says the well-meaning friend, "maybe this will help you." To which they reply, with sincere gratitude, "Lord knows I need a miracle." Thrilled to have found the truth, but not sure what to make of the Course's decidedly sophisticated style, eager new Course students might look for support either in their home town or on the Internet.

Anxious to resolve their problems, but not quite ready to accept their contribution to the one and only problem—a continued desire for an experience of separation—they seek out alternative interpretations of the Course, wanting the comfort of an approach that is less uncompromising, less bold, something that will make them feel better in the world. However, it usually doesn't take long before they come to the realization that this new spirituality is not going to solve their problems any time soon; disheartened, they wonder why their friend recommended this ridiculously complicated book in the first place, and on the shelf it goes. A few will return to it the very next day, the call being impossible to ignore; others, perhaps several years later, and still many more will never again open its cover.

And then there are those who are attracted to the Course simply because of its increasing popularity. So-and-so mentioned it in their blog, another referred to it in one of his books. Eager for a sense of belonging, they order their very own copy. Quickly joining the ranks of those baffled by its complexity as they attempt to read its very first pages, they too find a spot for it on a shelf, never to be read again. Sometimes, they give their copy away, usually to someone who is experiencing difficulty in their life. "Here, maybe this will help you," they say, happy to hand over the dusty blue book to their friend in need of a miracle. At least they can say that they know of the Course, maybe even say that they read it, long ago, perhaps even adding that it's a good book and they fully agree with what it says.

Many complain about the highly intellectual and sophisticated style of the Course, yet they have shelves full of books of all kinds, enough to baffle and confuse even the most highly intellectual person. These same people have no problem learning how to use remote controls, GPSs, cell phones, digital cameras, electronic gizmos and all manner of complicated and very confusing social media interfaces and computer applications.

Learning the theory of this spirituality is much like learning to read and write. Though memorizing the letters of the alphabet, learning the rules of grammar and learning to read "See spot run" was certainly not the highlight of anyone's early literary education, it sure came in handy as we grew up and began to experience and explore the big world away from home which required reading signs for bus routes or searching for our favourite recordings in music stores. Without this basic learning, there would be no "texting" nor "surfing the Net," not to mention the matter of learning to read the shorthand gibberish of those very same text messages. Since we all come from the same Source, we can begin with the assumption that, whether conscious of it or not, everyone wants peace of a lasting kind and, on a deeper level, everyone yearns to go home. However, not everyone—probably no one—is eager to look at the darkness that keeps us from the truth. For those who have been called to *A Course in Miracles* as their spiritual path, the simplest approach is to learn its alphabet, as best as possible, and then begin to apply it to the specific circumstances of their lives.

An essential aspect of Jesus' teaching method is that he speaks to us on two, distinct levels: as individual selves, seemingly in bodies, which is at the level of effect, and as spirit, with decision-making minds, which is at the level of cause. When he speaks to us as bodies, we are confused. "What do you mean, this is not my real home?" we reply, sometimes even indignantly. "I've worked hard to make it in the world. Besides, I'm here, in a body I can't deny, so this must be who I am!" When he speaks to us as spirit, he touches on our deepest yearning for the truth of our wholeness as God created us; he speaks to us where we actually are, with him, joined in mind, at a level of being we do not even know exists until someone points it out to us. "Come to where I am, awaken to where you really are, with me and all your brothers and sisters who are awake," he calls to us gently.

However, what is not immediately understood is that these levels are not connected in a linear fashion; rather they have a holographic relationship, which means that when the mind is ready, when the separated soul desires to experience its true state of wholeness, the level of cause can be reached instantaneously, without delays or impediments of any kind. Time is only real to the separated mind, believing itself to be trapped in a body. Until this relationship between the levels is understood, it is difficult to imagine that a shift from one level to the other is even possible, making the journey home appear interminably long. There is no hierarchy of spirituality; there is really no need for us to develop or perfect ourselves. The knowledge of our perfection is simply there, awaiting our remembering, since it is our natural state.

As long as we identify with the limited perception of our bodies and brains, we cannot but continue to believe that there are forces outside ourselves—outside our minds—that are the causes of all things, including our lives and the entire universe. This helps sustain the belief that we are powerless to affect change or to make progress on this journey. To the untrained mind, the only explanation that makes sense is that we are the victims of forces beyond our control. The Course helps us to change all that by showing us where true power lies: in the mind. The destination of this learning program—the return of the mind to wholeness—is also the starting point from which we came to believe it was possible to be separate from our Source, and so our journey, like a circle, will inevitably take us home. What is unnatural—the thought system of separation—cannot forever last; what is natural—perfect oneness—has never changed. It is what is referred to in the Course as a journey without distance.

Guilt: Our Dirty Little Secret

A Course in Miracles is a mind-training program designed to be applied in the mind and by the mind. Its goal is to correct our limited, faulty perceptions. But then, while Jesus maintains that the Course is practical, he also tells us that our eyes don't see and our brains don't think, the world we perceive, and all things in it—including the big blue book that we think is so important—do not even exist. He also tells us that we have been badly taught, besides which, we really don't know anything about anything. We are dreamers in a dream of our own making, seemingly far removed from reality, cut off from the true power of mind, in fact, we are mindless. So much for years of spiritual seeking!

So, how the heck are we supposed to look? What exactly does he want us to look at? And if our eyes don't see, how are we supposed to see? If we are asleep, who is supposed to be doing the looking? If there is a self that is not asleep, where is it? Where is this mind that he tells us needs training? What is this self? Can it see? What can it see? Who is Jesus talking to? Good grief, who is it that is asking all of these questions?

To add to our confusion, we are told that our minds are not out there in the world any more than we are out there in the world in bodies. If we truly want to see, there is no way to turn but inwards, something that is really quite simple and requires that we turn our attention around, one hundred eighty degrees. It is simple, except for the small matter of the barrier that stands between our identification with ourselves as individuals in bodies and the truth of the right mind that is hidden by the silly separation situation. At the core of our acceptance of the thought of separation is our belief in sin and the overwhelming guilt that this thought engenders. Guilt is essential to our maintaining the illusion of a separated self; without guilt, there is no need to hide or to maintain a state of separation. In oneness, there is no specialness, no conflict, no struggle for survival, there are no needs whatsoever. It is guilt that makes the world go round; not money, and certainly not love. In fact, it is guilt that made the world we see. Look no further for the cause of the world and our captivating experiences as seemingly separated bodies. Guilt is our dirty little secret, and now addicted to our state of separation, independent from the Father, it is a secret we cherish and cling to dearly.

> Of one thing you were sure: Of all the many causes you perceived as bringing pain and suffering to you, your guilt was not among them. (T-27.VII.7:4)

Since this statement about our belief in guilt is not likely to be a big crowd-pleaser, Jesus cuts us some slack, knowing full well that, at least in the beginning of our journey, we need to take small steps. So he draws us in, slowly, gently and lovingly, never judging us for our resistance, and above all, respecting our fear. After laying out the concepts of sin, guilt and fear, he reassures us by referring to our imagined barrier to the truth as being nothing more than a veil, something with no more substance than a feather, something that is really not a big deal. The whole thing is little more than a mistake, not even a sin, nor a crime, just a crazy idea, an idea that we once took seriously, but which we now should laugh at.

> This heavy-seeming barrier, this artificial floor that looks like rock, is like a bank of low dark clouds that seem to be a solid wall before the sun. Its impenetrable appearance is wholly an illusion. It gives way softly to the mountain tops that rise above it, and has no power at all to hold back anyone willing to

climb above it and see the sun. It is not strong enough to stop a button's fall, nor hold a feather. Nothing can rest upon it, for it is but an illusion of a foundation. Try but to touch it and it disappears; attempt to grasp it and your hands hold nothing. (T-18.IX.6)

However, as we begin to explore and bravely put into practice the Course's message of forgiveness, the ego, always eager to participate, is likely to join us on the journey. In fact, you can bet your big blue book that the ego will be right there with you, every step of the way. It has a vested interest in everything we do, especially where mind training is concerned, since its survival depends on our not re-training our minds to look anywhere but outwards. So long as we remain focused on the world of bodies, we remain mindless. Mindlessness is good, saith the ego. Mindlessness buys me some time. Time is great too; it keeps things moving forward in an illusory linear fashion. Time says there is a past in which I have sinned that will inevitably catch up with me in some undetermined future, thereby breeding fear. Mindlessness plus time; the perfect combo, ideal for ensuring that we continue to believe in the illusion!

Naturally, as we scratch beneath the surface of our slick, shiny ego-sculpted selves, we are bound to encounter resistance. There is one thing that is an absolute in the illusion: the ego does not have our best interests at heart. When we make our first attempts at turning our attention inwards, it gets nervous, and that thin veil Jesus talks about shows up as a solid brick wall. This is when we stumble and falter, and we begin to doubt that the Course will work for us. And we have barely begun our journey home!

While we bravely march forward on our journey, resistance begins to express itself in increasingly creative and clever ways, such as an increased interest in work, a growing addiction to surfing the Internet, an influx of endless external activities, obligations and distractions, and we forget to read our lessons, and what we have learned about forgiveness somehow never makes its way into our awareness as we go about our daily activities. Besides which, this blue book is so hard to read! So it is that we end up exclaiming that the Course is too difficult!

Look Ma, No Guilt!

But what if I don't experience any guilt? A common question—a statement, really—inspired by: you guessed it, our friendly neighbourhood ego, always ready to make us feel better about ourselves, our separated selves, that is. This is a statement often expressed by beginning students who have "worked on themselves" for many years. But I don't feel guilty! I've dealt with all that stuff from the past; I've forgiven my rotten, cheating spouse, my abusive parent, my ungrateful children, for what he, she, or they did to me. It's all in the past now. It's over and done with. Besides which, it's all an illusion anyways, so why look for guilt!

Evidently, since guilt is at the heart of each and every person's secret beliefs about themselves, all that hard work has not taken them deeply enough. It may have led to much personal growth and improved self-understanding, clearly an important part of the process of spiritual awakening, but it has not led to the core of the problem. For the long-time spiritual seeker who is open and ready for the message of the Course—but at the same time, who's ego is just a touch hyper-sensitive—a common response is to simply deny the guilt and the rest of the darkness that lurks beneath the surface, hiding the sordid mess behind the shiny veneer of pretty spiritual and metaphysical morsels of wisdom. The truth is that, the guilt we feel is so horrible, that no one is in touch with it, at least not willingly. No one wants to go there. Ignorance is the ego's safety net, and since we are effectively mindless, we do not see that there is another way of looking.

> Sin is a block, set like a heavy gate, locked and without a key, across the road to peace. No one who looks on it without the help of reason would try to pass it. The body's eyes behold it as solid granite, so thick it would be madness to attempt to pass it. Yet reason sees through it easily, because it is an error. The form it takes cannot conceal its emptiness from reason's eyes. (T-22.III.3:2–6)

Why do we need to look at this guilt? Is it not enough just to know that it is there? If we don't feel guilty, and we feel peaceful, why bother digging it up? Why bother making waves? Don't we have enough drama and conflict to deal with in our lives already? Isn't peace the goal? Well, if there were no guilt, we would not be here; and if there were no guilt and we were here, then we would be immune to the condition of misperceptionitis, enjoying a per-ennial state of unalterable peace, wholeness, joy and total love for absolutely everyone and everything all the time. We would know that there is nothing that lies outside the presence of God.

Belief in guilt is essential to the survival of the ego; without which there would be no fear of looking within. To begin to look at the guilt is to begin the process of undoing this wrong-minded thought system—the lie that says that what God created can be sinful. Do we need to ferret out every single guilty thought we have ever harboured? Because that could take a lifetime and more. No! Absolutely not. What we need is to become wise to the ego's antics, to become familiar enough with its clever ways of keeping us from uncovering the truth of our wholeness so we can catch it in the act. We need to recognize the guilt as it arises so we can say "no," the Son of God is not sinful. To let go of the guilt is to be ready to accept that we are—all of us—sinless, as God created us, therefore without any need to hide in a make-believe world. To let go of the guilt is to abandon the false self and allow the true Self to express the Glory of God.

A New Way of Looking

We may have asked for another way of looking, but we probably didn't expect that we would be required to give up our old way of looking—a way that tells us that there is nothing beyond form and that we are limited to the bodies in which we appear to be encased. We are now being asked to look with the eyes of our sane, right mind, eyes that are not blinded by form, shape or colour, nor by false teachings or pictures of past memories. When we look with eyes that capture and transmit light impulses to the brain—the artificial light of an illusory world—we are looking with an instrument of the wrong mind, with eyes that don't see. We are being invited now to be curious about what lies beyond the darkness we experience with our limited sight. What is it that we are not seeing?

> These eyes, made not to see, will never see. For the idea they represent left not its maker, and it is their maker that sees through them. What was its maker's goal but not to see? For this the body's eyes are perfect means, but not for seeing. See how the body's eyes rest on externals and cannot go beyond. Watch how they stop at nothingness, unable to go beyond the form to meaning. Nothing so blinding as perception of form. For sight of form means understanding has been obscured. (T-22.III.6:1–8)

When we look with the true vision of forgiveness—without judgment, unaffected by any perception of differences—we are looking with our right mind. We are asked to set aside the impressions of the senses that report back pictures in a dream and choose instead the light of true vision that sees that we are all the same, sons and

Looking with Jesus

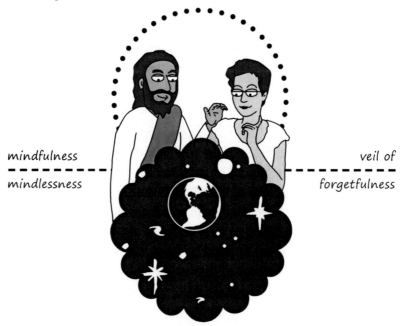

mindfulness

mindlessness

veil of

forgetfulness

daughters of God, whole and loved by our Father. In our practice, we are simply asked to be vigilant for our thoughts, our decisions, our reactions and our delinquent mind-wanderings. This will tell us how we have chosen to look.

Since the cost of letting go of our guilt is the relinquishment of this false, limited self-perception with which we so staunchly and willingly identify, it is wise to employ an approach that will not generate unnecessary fear or anxiety. The only way to look at this darkness that we have worked so hard at maintaining as a barrier to the truth is to stand back and look at it with someone who will not judge us, someone kind, understanding, gentle and loving, someone who will not add to our guilt when we mess up—and we *will* mess up—someone who does not buy into the silly, mad idea, someone like Jesus, who has awakened from the dream. Only in this way can we look without being overwhelmed by fear. Only then can we appreciate what this mistaken choice has cost us—the experience of the Love of God—and only then can we make the decision to let it go.

At least at the beginning of our journey to wholeness, we don't need to do much other than be willing to accept that perhaps we have been wrong in our way of looking and to ask for help in seeing things differently. We must then trust that we will receive the help we need to make this shift in perception. Our bodies were designed to transmit data from within the world of form, thus keeping our attention perpetually focused on the world, away from the part of the mind with which we continuously make decisions. From within our worldly experience, we are essentially mindless, that is, disconnected from the level of mind that has the power to make changes of any kind.

The world we see is little more than a senseless, make-believe battleground we call our home away from home. It is what we see when we suffer from misperceptionitis, a limited way of seeing that makes the world seem real. In truth, there is only the illusion of a battleground. How could God allow His children to fight for survival in a world that leads only to death? He could not, and He does not. What God creates lives forever, in complete abundance, in the safety of perfect oneness. If His children experience a battleground, it is because this is what they have chosen to experience. While the children have chosen to close their eyes and play a while in a made-up world, the Kingdom of Heaven remains unchanged; it is simply temporarily hidden by the illusory made-up world.

> See no one from the battleground, for there you look on him from nowhere. You have no reference point from where to look, where meaning can be given what you see. (T-23.IV.7:1–2)

Though we may have chosen to experience this battleground of a life, we are not required to engage in, or accept, every battle with which we seem to be confronted. We are not asked to be war heroes. We do not have to walk through the entire battlefield in order to return to the wholeness of the Kingdom of Heaven. There is a way that is much quicker, much more effective, and above all, much less painful. Instead, we are invited to simply rise above it. No one receives special medals in Heaven for needless suffering, pain, and war wounds. On the contrary, to choose to persist in engaging in battle is to delay our return home to a life of eternal peace and wholeness. To continue to choose for an illusory experience is to deny the full expression of wholeness that is the birthright of each and every one of God's children. It is to refuse to accept what the Father Wills for His children.

As a way of pulling my attention out of the ego's clutches, I found it helpful to stand back, sometimes imagining myself reeling my mind way back from the situation until I sensed that I had risen far enough above the conflict so that I could begin to see it clearly. By rising above the battleground, we are in touch with our right mind, no longer blinded by the darkness of the world of form, less likely to be influenced by the ego's interpretation of events. From this new vantage point, we can look at any situation without judgment, fear or anxiety, because we know that it is not real. From this new vantage point, we know that all of our brothers have the same ability to rise above the battleground and come to that place in the mind that is safe and whole, where we join as one. We see now only expressions of love, or calls for love.

Whenever we experience conflict of any kind, our battle really is with ourselves. It is the battle between the small, separated self with which we identify, the self we recognize in the bathroom mirror every morning, and the Self that is part of the whole, the Self that knows only love. While we seem to do battle a little while longer, we might ask: What is its purpose? There is no battleground; there is no battle. There is only a clinging to the guilt that comes from a desire to be separate from the Father, thus necessitating a battleground onto which it can be projected.

While to persist in looking at our life situations from within the battleground may lead to an excellent understanding of life in a world filled with ongoing battles, it will not lead us home. This means that as long as we see only form, differences, shades, colours, shapes, sizes, we cannot truly see. We are blinded by the forms of an illusory battleground. To see with the eyes of true vision requires that we change our perspective, and the only true perspective can come as we raise our awareness above the world of form in which we seem to live and become curious about experiencing the truth that lies beyond, the Kingdom of Heaven that is right here, right now.

From Darkness to Light

Every day we groom and dress ourselves to meet the requirements of our various activities. Certain outfits are appropriate for work while others are more suited to evening-wear. We probably would not wear a designer suit to wash the car, or stiletto heels to climb a mountain. Each time we dress ourselves, it is with a certain purpose; we seek to present the right look for a particular occasion. On the way out, we check our appearance in the mirror just to verify that we have achieved the desired result. We might tweak a collar, straighten out a skirt hem or adjust a cuff just so the image we see is to our satisfaction. The mirror tells us what we need to know.

In a similar way, the entire universe and all things in it acts as a gigantic mirror. However, this mirror reflects back to us what we hold to be true about ourselves on a deep, unconscious level. This mirror remains with us at all times and serves to provide invaluable information about our inner wish—the true cause of our experiences—the decision for separation, or for wholeness. Moreover, since what we do not wish to see about ourselves—our secret sins and hidden fears—needs to be projected externally, we also actively, albeit unconsciously, set out to find suitable mirrors for projection. When we project our secret sins and hidden fears onto our brothers, we preserve our innocence and also push away the Love of God. This is the ego's favourite sport.

We are now being taught to awaken that part of our mind that is beyond the brain that processes perceptual data, that part of the mind that knows that nothing can hurt or harm that which is whole. From this new perspective, it becomes clear that to see anything other than a call for love or an expression of love is to choose to push away love. When we see anything but wholeness, it is because this is what we have chosen to see, and so we have chosen with our wrong mind.

Looked at from above the battleground, it becomes clear that there are no battles worth fighting, there is never any justification for conflict in the world. It is our own call for love that we see projected out into the world, and at the same time, our great fear of truly accepting this love, for its acceptance is also the acceptance of our oneness and the denial of separation. Standing above the battleground, looking with Jesus, we see clearly that we are never upset for the reason we think; and we can always choose peace instead. Our brothers are either expressing love, or they are calling for love.

By training ourselves to become mindful of our perceptions, we can learn to recognize with which thought system we have chosen to experience a particular person or situation. A very simple way to know how we have chosen is by the outcome: if we are at peace, we likely have chosen with the right mind; if not, well, there is only one other possible choice. There are many spiritualities that share the process of looking, of being the observer, but unlike these teachings, the Course does not ask us to change our thoughts, modify our behaviour, or atone for our past mistakes. Nor does the practice of being vigilant for our thoughts involve extensive analysis of events and situations going on in the world, in our minds or in our lives. We are asked only to observe and acknowledge that what we see is what we have chosen to witness, and if we find it difficult to look, we are invited to look with a kind and non-judgmental teacher, the Holy Spirit, or Jesus.

What this new way of looking requires of us is a little—okay, a lot—of willingness to look honestly. Why do we need to look at our

darkness? Our fears? Our hatred and our judgments? If we cover them up with nice thoughts about ourselves and hide behind nice behaviour, how will we ever know of the darkness that obscures the full light of our true nature? For the same reason, we are asked to be grateful for the opportunities to see the darkness, without which we would never know of its existence. It is only by looking at the darkness, without judgment, without fear, that we can pierce through the seemingly solid dark wall of sin, guilt and fear, and see it for the nothing that it is. We are now beginning to awaken that part of our mind that is beyond the brain that processes perceptual data, that part of the mind in which the power of choice resides.

To be in the right mind is to know that separation is impossible, and that it has never occurred. It is to experience with absolute certainty the calm and peace of knowing that the children of God have never left the Kingdom of Heaven. To be in the right mind is to see that there is no error, no sin, no guilt nor any need to fear punishment; it is to be able to overlook all symbols and representations of separation such as specialness, hatred, anger, defensiveness, and attack.

A right mind cannot be attacked, hurt or disturbed in any way. In the right mind, thoughts of judgment are impossible; free of the impulse to judge, the right mind is peaceful. Since peace is a condition for entering the Kingdom of Heaven, to be in the right mind is to meet the condition for the return home. Right-minded living means to live in wholeness, safety and joy, knowing that we are whole, invulnerable, loved as God created us. There is no fear, no need, no anxiety, no urgency; there is only love, safety, peace.

As we practise looking with the right mind, the wall that blocks the light of truth begins to weaken and eventually begins to crumble. This is a practice, one that requires the conscious application of choice and dedication to the process. It's not what we see with our eyes that matters, it's how we look with our mind, and what we do with what we see that matters. In other words, it's how we interpret what we see that matters. How we look will determine how we will interpret what we see. If we look with our right mind, from above the battleground, from a place where judgment is inconceivable, where lies the remembrance of the truth of our oneness, we will see the truth.

The darkness is not true. It only seems to be true to those of us who fear the light. The darkness is a state of our own choosing. It is not a necessary or a required condition. If we do not know the light, or do not remember our enlightenment, it is because we do not wish to know it at this time. The time we take for remembrance is up to each and every one of us. The time we take is not important for it is not real. At any moment, we can make a different choice, but first, we must become aware of the fact that we always have the power to choose, and our choice is what determines our experience at any given moment.

Chapter 10

THE QUIET MIND

Knowledge is not the motivation for learning this course. Peace is. This is the prerequisite for knowledge only because those who are in conflict are not peaceful, and peace is the condition of knowledge because it is the condition of the Kingdom. (T-8.I.1:1–3)

The Importance of Peace

*T*HE GOAL OF *A Course in Miracles* is peace. It's not love, world peace, escape from hardship, the eradication of suffering, healing, abundance for all, business or professional success, or a greener earth. The goal of the Course is simply peace. Peace is nice, you might say. I want peace. Most people I meet would claim that they want peace. However, since our experiences are the outcomes of our choices, if we truly wanted peace, we would have peace. Clearly, if we are not at peace, it is because we have not chosen it, proving that we prefer to experience something else instead. In the end, we have the experience we desire.

Those who still value goals such as professional success, a special relationship, money, power, fame, success, and whose attention is primarily focused on the attainment of these goals, may find it difficult, at least at first, to reconcile the non-worldly goal of the Course with these mundane goals. At some point, these values will be put into question and re-examined for their true worth, and the desire to hold onto them may result in some feelings of conflict or confusion. Hence the reason why a spirituality such as *A Course in Miracles* is more suited for those who, a bit later in life, have just about exhausted their valueless worldly ambitions and are ready to explore something new.

The peace of God is not the seeming peace that comes from winning an argument, being right or acquiring something. These are forms of ego satisfaction, since they are based on me or the other; someone gains, someone loses. When all appears well, when things seem to be running smoothly, when life is relatively conflict-free, very often it is simply that we are experiencing temporary respite from the burden of maintaining our unnatural belief in separation from perfect oneness intact and inaccessible. By throwing us a crumb now and then, the ego does take good care of its minions! Add a little conflict, mess up a beautiful day with an unexpected thunderstorm, or worse, a computer crash, and see how quickly peace disappears. Which means that peace that is based on happenings in the world is relative, and therefore cannot be true. If it is not constant and unchanging, it is not the peace of God.

Why is peace so important? For those who have concluded, or even just sensed, that this world cannot be our real home, that there must be something else, peace is very important. Lasting peace is not found in this world, a lesson often learned only in the school of hard knocks. Peace is important for those who want to go home, because peace is a condition of the Kingdom. Only a mind that is devoid of even the slightest hint of conflict can enter the Kingdom of Heaven, for there, conflict cannot enter. As long as one spot of darkness remains, the smallest hint of guilt, shame, anger, resentment or fear, we cannot enter the Kingdom. Darkness, conflict, lack of peace are reflected in the choices we make on a daily basis, showing up in how we see our brothers, hence the importance for being vigilant for our thoughts while we are busy in the world.

Peace comes from choosing with the Holy Spirit; conflict comes from choosing with the ego. Peace does not come from what is going on outside your mind, in the world. To want the peace of God *and* something else, is to be in conflict; peace will not be found, for to want anything but peace is to believe in scarcity or lack. All my clients claim that they want peace. However, when we explore those difficult situations for which they seek resolution—and peace—it becomes clear that the peace they want comes with conditions. If only he would stop yelling; if only they took my opinions seriously; if only they would clean up their rooms; if only my boss wasn't such a jerk; if only the economy was better; if only we had better schools; if only my candidate were elected; if only… if only… if only… I would be at peace. Under those conditions, peace will not be found. If our state of peace depended on external circumstances, there would be no hope, for what is outside is what we believe to be true inside our minds. In order to have peace, it must come from within; it is a decision only we can make, in our mind.

You may, on the other hand, have managed to set up your life so that you generally experience a peaceful existence; it has become a lifestyle choice. Or you may, as in my case, have been born with a natural aversion to open conflict, which, since the ego is generally in charge until it gets ousted as director of what goes on in our mind, simply causes the conflict to be refocused internally, either mentally, emotionally or physically. To exist as an individual, separate from our Source, is an unnatural act, and must produce conflict on some level. Being introspective by nature, it wasn't long before I was able to quickly recognize my external button-pushers, after which I engaged in the practice of standing back, looking with my Teacher, and, as soon as possible, choosing peace instead. The big stuff was rather quickly and easily identified and dealt with.

It was the little things that caught me by surprise. Being more of a big-picture person than a detail-oriented person, I had been overlooking those little, daily, seemingly insignificant bumps. Like the garbage can at the end of the kitchen counter that frequently competed for space with my left foot as I hustled into the kitchen for that important cup of tea, food for my cat Maggie, a quick lunch before a consult—all the important little details of life that kept me mindlessly running about—causing a colourful expletive to arise, thereby very quickly and effectively erasing my cherished peace. As I became more aware of these seemingly innocuous peace-robbing events—and there were a few throughout a normal day—I made it a point to catch myself before snapping. In time, actually, a very short time, when these small things arose, instead, I smiled. They were very silly, and certainly not worth giving up my peace over. This vigilance for the small stuff further contributed to my appreciation for choosing peace as the sane alternative. More peace, less ego!

In peace, there is only wholeness; there cannot be a need for anything else. Since peace is our natural condition, its attainment must be effortless. For those who are committed to undoing the ego and awakening to the truth, peace is the weapon of choice. Peace is to the ego what kryptonite is to Superman. When peace is chosen, the mind is clear and inspiration and guidance can be more easily received. As our appreciation for this state of peace grows, we are likely to choose it more frequently. As peace becomes the normal condition, the ego's power fades and we become instruments of what is right-minded.

Thanks for the Invitation, but… No Thanks!

"Well, depends on how you look at it." How often have you said these words when asked to weigh in on an issue? And what do they mean, exactly? Isn't looking just looking? Doesn't everyone see the same thing when they look at the same thing? Why can't people agree when faced with the same circumstance? When we see with the body's eyes, our brain will associate the image of our perception with some learning from the past, all of which leads to interpretation. Since each person's past is a unique combination of learning and experience, each person will return a unique interpretation of a given situation. For example, a picture of a bridge might stir feelings of adventure when associated with an enjoyable road trip taken as a child with Mom and Dad, sister Donna and Dingbat the family dachshund; the same picture might stir panic and overwhelming guilt in someone who watched their boyfriend commit suicide by jumping off the old abandoned bridge at the edge of town.

Unless and until we train ourselves to look differently, all of our perceptions are filtered through, and therefore tainted by the lens of our past experiences. This the ego uses to keep us anchored in the belief that something outside of us can cause us to feel joy, happiness, grief or anxiety. Without a past, the bridge is simply a steel structure spanning a waterway. Without a past, each experience can be perceived as something new. A mind that is at peace is more likely to see a situation as it is, untainted by the past, free of the ego's interpretations, and therefore in a better position to respond according to the true need, which, more often than not, is a call for love.

> The ego's way is not mine, but it is also not yours. The Holy Spirit has one direction for all minds, and the one He taught me is yours. Let us not lose sight of His direction through illusions, for only illusions of another direction can obscure the one for which God's Voice speaks in all of us. Never accord the ego the power to interfere with the journey. (T-8.V.6:1–4)

The ego is always on the lookout for clever and innovative ways of grabbing our attention, something it must do because its survival depends on our attentiveness. If we ignore it, then it will not appear to exist; at least, it will not have the power it appears to have, which really means that we give it power when we give it our attention. *But don't tell the ego we have this part figured out; it is likely to lash out at you!* In order to sustain our attention, it is constantly sending out invitations. To ensure that we will accept its invitations, the ego makes it a point to become well acquainted with all of our special button-pushers, our weaknesses, our insecurities, our fears—everything it needs to prepare invitations that are nearly impossible for us to refuse.

A master at sales and marketing, the ego knows just how to close a deal, sweetening the pot according to our weaknesses and addictions, with just the right enticement. It will promise satisfaction and joy from being right, getting something from a brother, winning a battle; or it will promise that we will feel extra special, that we will be loved, that we will not feel lonely or afraid, or that we will forget about our suffering and our pain for a while. It will derive great satisfaction when, at the same time, we get to project some of our repressed sin, guilt or fear onto someone or something else. Being right *and* pointing the finger at someone for doing something wrong is an ego jackpot!

Invitations from the ego come in countless forms; many of them impossible to ignore. It says, look at what your brother has done. And, in looking, you see that your brother has cut you off in line where you stood, quietly waiting to order your morning coffee and muffin. At this time, as at all times, in each and every moment, you have two choices: you are free to rise above the battleground, see your brother whole, as God created him, lost in a dream and momentarily ignorant of his truth, at which point you may intuit that perhaps he is in a hurry, he may be on his way to the hospital or be caught up in some emergency or other. Perhaps he was too shy to ask permission to step into the line, or, perhaps he was distracted. It may very well be that he is simply lacking in social grace. No matter your brother's circumstance, you remain free to choose to keep your peace, or not; he has not done anything to you.

Ever vigilant and eager to jump on any opportunity that might reinforce and help sustain its weaselly existence, the ego will have another perspective on the same situation, one that will have as its purpose the supplanting of your exasperating sense of peace. It will invite you to see your brother as being annoying, rude and inconsiderate, an opportunity to forget the whole silly idea of peace and to choose conflict instead. *Defend your spot in line; you were here first; stand up for your rights; come on, don't be such a wuss; what will people think! You're going to be late for work because of this guy's rudeness.* As indignation stirs, and you begin to feel a little hot under the collar, you know you have accepted the ego's invitation to see your brother as he is not, to see him as the cause of your upset, when the truth is that, all the while, it was up to you to choose to remain at peace, or to become upset. If you are upset, it is not because of what a brother did; it is because you accepted the ego's invitation to be upset. Becoming upset means you are no longer at peace; you're off to a great start for another day in ego-mode, and the ego wins another round.

Throughout our days and nights, we are constantly being bombarded with invitations. When we feel angry, impatient, resentful, fearful, defensive—when we experience any form of upset or lack of peace—it is because we have accepted the ego's invitation. Once caught up in the emotion, you may feel you have, once again, failed. It appears as though you will never return to your right mind; not only have you lost your peace, you are now disappointed in yourself for having failed in your spiritual pursuit. Not true. The thought that you have failed is an attempt made by the ego to infiltrate your mind and convince you that you are less than what you truly are: the son or daughter of God, whole, as God created you. If you are looking at your thoughts, you are in your right mind, and therefore have not failed.

And if you are still stuck with a lingering, unwanted thought, fear not, it is always time to say: stop! We are not expected to get it right the first time, nor the tenth, nor the hundredth time. If we did, then we wouldn't need the big blue book. We are asked simply to try, until we get it right. As thoughts of anger, impatience or failure arise—for they are only thoughts—say to yourself with authority: I no longer wish to engage this thought of anger, resentment, fear, impatience. Stop! Say it aloud, if you like; only, say it like you mean it. Stop! Then go do something else; go get a glass of water, go for a walk, dance around the room until the thought is gone. Go eat a cookie.

Thoughts are habits and habits can be changed. When an "unholy" thought arises and threatens to upset my peace, I flip an imaginary switch in my mind. *Stop!* I say. I am the boss of my mind; I have the power to choose which Teacher I will follow. If I chose with the wrong mind in the first place, I can just as easily choose with the right mind now. By flipping the switch, I am diminishing the power of my wrong mind to determine my experience. I am creating and strengthening a new habit: yes to right-mindedness. Yes to peace. Yes to wholeness. Yes to love.

The Nature of Mind

Each and every one of us is a thought in the Mind of God. The Mind of God is purely creative. What comes from the Mind of God is like God: whole, perfect, and creative. When we decided to run outside and play on our own and try our hand at being separate and independent from our Father, we abandoned our true nature of wholeness, perfection and creativity. A mind that believes itself separate from the Mind of God has no true power. While we pretend to be separate, we can no longer tap into the creative energy of the Mind of God. Instead, what we are left with is the uncreative power of imagination. As separate, independent minds, the best we can do is imagine things that might be. Under the guidance of the ego, we can only imagine things that are untrue. We cannot create things that are true. Imagination has no real life force; it is little more than a make-believe creativity. As marvellous and as wonderful as our make-believe world appears to be, even in its most glorious expressions, it remains a poor substitute for the glory of the true creation of God.

The separated mind is like a bent and cracked branch that no longer receives its full share of sap and life force from its parent, the tree. In its broken form, the branch must struggle to survive; without the flow of the life force of the tree, it must suffer the loss of what little life it seems to have, and in time, inevitable death. If the branch is straightened out and temporarily wrapped with a binding cloth and supported where it was bent, it can, with the help of the flow of life from the tree, begin to mend. Once mended, it now resumes life as an integral part of the tree. It is no longer a separate, struggling branch; it is once again part of a living whole.

To be asleep and experiencing a dream is to believe it possible to exist apart from the flow of life; it is to believe that being bent is normal. Likewise, when we look through the eyes of a mind that believes in separation, our perception is bent; it no longer truly sees. It can only see what is bent; it sees a body that is separate from the whole. It sees other bodies that are separate from the whole. It cannot perceive wholeness. In order to return our mind to true perception, we must go back to that point where the mind is bent into believing that it is possible to be separate. As we begin to enable correct perception, the flow of the life that is our true inheritance, the life that is whole, eternal and creative, the life that is our birthright, begins to flow through us once more. This is the beginning of healing; this is the beginning of awakening; this is the beginning of our return to everlasting Being.

The ongoing busyness of the separated mind is little more than a childish and ineffectual attempt at reproducing the creative ability of the real Mind of which we are an integral part. To attempt to control and stop the flow of this busyness is like trying to stop the flow of water from a broken water main by pushing the water back from the sidewalk with our bare hands. The only way to stop the flow of water is to shut off the water at its source and repair the break. Once repaired, we can again control the flow of water for its intended purpose.

Likewise, if we wish to control or stop the flow of busyness in the mind, we must return to that still, quiet centre where we first chose against peace. This is the point at which we chose to experience ourselves as separate, autonomous entities, seemingly capable of functioning apart from our Source. To return to that still, quiet centre in the mind is to be willing to relinquish our false creative power, to abandon authorship of our dream, knowing that all we can do as sleeping minds is imagine empty dreams. Without a deep sense that there is something better than the dream of separation, the giving up of this authorship can, for most seekers, be frightening, hence the need for a gentle, progressive approach.

A mind that is not quiet is incapable of right thinking. The question to be asked when one is finding difficulty quieting the mind is, Why do I want a noisy mind? Perhaps I do not want right thinking. Again, to not want right thinking is to protect the ego's interests. The quiet mind is a condition that is a threat to the ego. Understanding that this is a choice we have made and wanting to access the wisdom of our right mind, it becomes easier to make the mind quiet.

When faced with situations in which we are feeling any form of indecision or uncertainty, we are attempting to figure things out on our own, without guidance. In order to hear guidance the mind must be quiet. Independent wilfulness must be abandoned and replaced with acceptance, surrender, and an expectation that our request for guidance will be answered. Only then can guidance come. To approach any situation independently is to join with the ego, which means we are coming from a place of fear. True guidance can only come with the relinquishment of the desire to be self-governing, autonomous and independent from our Source.

There is no sanity in thinking independently from the Father. To think it possible to exist independently of the Father is the source of the problem of separation and can only bring grief, sorrow, pain and incompleteness. Independent thinking is insane. It is not sane because it is not whole. It does not serve the greater good, and therefore cannot serve our good. Independent thinking leads to indecision, conflict, uncertainty, fear and lack of satisfaction because it is not supported by what is true, whole, or natural. To decide to give up independent thinking is the first step towards sanity. To allow the Will of the Father to replace independent thinking is what places us in the flow of creation. That is true power. There is no real power in independent thinking. The sole purpose of independent thinking is to block out the truth.

The Mind of God is the only Source of life, love and creativity. Until it is turned over to the Holy Spirit, what we know of as intellect is used mostly for the purpose of the ego and is used for independent thinking. There is no independent thinking in the Mind of God. In order to allow God's expression to flow through us, faith in independent thinking must be relinquished. Faith in independent thinking is faithlessness. All freedom comes from abandoning independent thought. All joy comes from allowing God's expression.

When I first realized what exactly this meant—the actual abandonment of my cherished personal will and independent mind—I panicked. This was going to be a very scary shift for my ego-attached mind, but I was determined to see it through. Flipping the switch on the ego, I decided to move forward. What did I have to lose? My wilfulness? My over-active, independent, overly analytical mind? As frightening as all this seemed, and I knew that only my ego could experience fear, the thought of abandoning my treasured independence was intriguing, bringing with it a sense of great relief. If I gave up my independent will, and asked instead, Father, what is Thy Will? I would not have to struggle so much with the almost incessant complicated decisions of the world. I would experience greater peace, and above all, greater freedom. This issue was further clarified in an early morning message.

"When in a state of indecision, tossing around two or three options, you are in your own separated individual mind and working from individual will. The problem is not that there appears to be a choice between multiple options. That is not the problem. The problem is that you are attached to your individual will, thinking that you can make decisions apart from the Will of the Father. By abandoning individual will, you allow guidance that is more knowledgeable than your individual will to enter. Individual will serves the individual, therefore, the ego. True guidance serves all."

Our minds are constantly churning out all manner of thoughts. How can we tell a wrong-minded thought from a right-minded thought? Any thought that carries with it an expectation that what we say or do in the world will bring us joy or wholeness or satisfaction of some kind comes from the wrong mind. Wrong-minded thoughts are based on the belief that the world has something of value, and what we do in the world is important for what it gives. Wrong-minded thoughts reflect a belief in differences and hierarchies of illusions, and lead to judgment. Wrong-minded thoughts maintain the illusion of separation and never lead to lasting peace.

A right-minded thought is not attached to an expectation of receiving joy from what happens in the world. True joy comes from the knowledge that nothing of this world can substitute for, nor circumvent the love, the joy, and the peace of God. Thoughts that come from the right mind come from a place of peace and wholeness, they are non-judgmental and all-inclusive in nature, and therefore can only inspire acts that are kind and loving. The best way to learn about how our mind works is to be vigilant for our thoughts, from the moment we wake up in the morning until we go to sleep at night.

Easing into the Practice of Meditation

Being created equal, by the same Father, everyone has the same properties of mind; we can choose to awaken to our true creative reality, or we can choose to remain asleep and continue to pretend to live in our imaginary world. No one has a better mind or a greater ability to control their mind than anyone else. Each person's ability to control the mind is a reflection of their choice of Teacher. The sometimes increasing noise in the mind of the sincere seeker is little more than an expression of the fear of going within. This awareness should be greeted with joy, as it indicates that progress is being made.

Many ask: How can I find the quiet centre in my mind when my mind is constantly busy? I have tried many forms of meditation, but none of them seem to work. I don't know how to turn off my thoughts. I try, and I try but the noise seems to get louder and busier. I will never be able to control my mind. I will never awaken from the dream. It seems hopeless! A better question to ask might be, What purpose does the noise serve? The world, including our bodies, and our brains that process thousands of bits of perceptual data every day, is designed to keep us mindless, that is, to keep us far from the quiet centre in our mind where true power resides.

The last thing the ego wants is for us to quiet the chattering monkeys in the insane jungle of our separated minds. A quiet mind is more likely to look inwards and in that quiet, it is ready to hear inner guidance. It is in the quiet mind that the truth is heard. Inner guidance spells competition for the ego, and so it will do whatever it takes to squash the competition. A more suitable form of practice, at least at the beginning, might be to simply observe the mind, noisy chatter and all. Watch the ego have its tantrum but do not allow it to disturb your peace. To fight or to attempt to control the ego's noisy outbursts is to give it power. To not take it seriously is to begin its undoing.

A client of mine was upset with her inability to rid herself of lingering thoughts about justifiably painful and traumatic experiences from her childhood. She was sincere in her devotion to her spiritual quest, having incorporated intensive yoga, Zen and meditation practices into her life, but she clearly felt she had little or no control over her mind. Finally she exclaimed, "But I am my ego!" And there was her answer: the reason why she was unable to quiet her mind was because she had accepted the ego's invitation to believe that she is what she is not: the ego. Believing herself to be her ego, there was no way for her to see that she had an alternative, that she had the power in her mind to choose between the wrong and the right mind and that she was the one choosing to believe the ego's lie. This was a significant breakthrough in her understanding of herself and her spiritual practice.

To be upset with yourself for a temporary inability to still the mind would be as silly as to be upset with the bent branch for hanging and losing its leaves and vitality. To battle with the wayward thoughts generated by a bent, misguided, misperceiving mind would not be an effective approach for bringing peace to the mind. Furthermore, to focus attention on thoughts alone is to give them more validity than they really need. Since peace is a condition for entering the Kingdom of Heaven, a battling mind will certainly not bring you closer to the goal.

To better understand the extent to which you are fearful of the quiet, try this exercise. Pick an evening where you have no obligations, where you have three hours to yourself, say a Friday evening. Turn off all the noise and potential sources of distraction: cell phones, television, computer. Don't post your intention on your social media page; don't text your BFF. Be uncompromising in this. We have many more opportunities for quiet meditation than we care to admit. Have a simple, light meal, no stimulants, no coffee or wine. Nothing you might blame for feeling uncomfortable. Set yourself up in a quiet room, with a comfortable chair. Since the way home is not found outside, but rather inside, in the mind, here is your opportunity to journey there. You can, if this is conducive to meditation, play some appropriate music softly in the background, but very softly. Make yourself comfortable; bring a blanket, a glass of water, some cushions. Just not too comfortable, since the point is to remain conscious; you don't want to fall asleep. Then sit with eyes closed, for as long as you can. Take occasional walks around the room or the house, in silence, as needed, to remain alert. Resist the urge to go to the computer or to check your text messages. Do not judge yourself as having failed if you are unable to remain in your quiet space for the full three hours. This exercise is meant as a way of appreciating the degree to which you fear the quiet.

For those who sincerely seek awakening to the presence of God, the quiet mind becomes a desired experience. With practice, quiet becomes a welcome and most natural alternative to noise. For those who have concluded that meditation is too difficult, it is possible to find alternative, even creative, means to cajole the mind into quietness. Walking in the woods, listening to soothing music, sitting by a gently flowing stream, deep breathing exercises, yoga, chanting, working in the garden, soaking in a hot bath, watching snowflakes swirl to the ground—these are all activities that can help foster an experience of quietness. Seek those activities that lead you to your experience of quiet and peace.

As appreciation for this state develops, a next step might be to sit quietly for five-minute periods, perhaps two or three times a day. Music geared for meditation, candlelight, the soothing sound of a small water fountain can help set the appropriate mood. With repeated practice, the quiet mind is nurtured and strengthened. As the desire to experience a peaceful mind grows, the ability to sit, walk, stand or just be in quiet stillness grows. The sense of peace and wholeness that comes with this state becomes a normal and even sought-after activity, just like eating, drinking or even breathing.

Connecting with Inner Guidance

Much like the bent branch of the tree that needs wrapping and support in order for it to mend, as children believing ourselves to be separate from our Father, we need support while we relinquish our dreams of separation. Any child desirous of awakening needs but reach out and ask for help. That help is found where it is needed; in the mind. It is only in the mind that perception can be corrected; it is in the quiet mind that true guidance is found. With dedicated practice and increased quiet, it is possible to open up to inner guidance, to become aware of a helping presence that is always available, a kind, loving and wise presence, ready to guide us on our journey of awakening. Since we are asleep in a dream, it is only logical—and natural—that there must be a place in our mind where we are awake. We can turn to this part of the mind for help.

In developing a relationship with inner guidance, at first it can be helpful to practise with simple questions, just to get the feel for how this guidance can be heard. I had one such occasion when a yoga mat I ordered online at Sears arrived at the designated pick up location, a dry cleaner in walking distance to my home. At the same time, I had also ordered a Sears Club rewards card which I planned to apply to the purchase at the time of pickup. The following day, I received a second notification that my order was ready for pickup, but the card had not arrived in the mail. I had a minor situation: I wanted to apply the ten dollars to my order, but I did not have the card; if the card did not arrive within the next twelve days, the mat would be returned and a restocking fee would be applied. It was not a big deal; I could pick up the mat and use the card on something else, but as I did not make frequent purchases at Sears, the card was likely to expire beforehand. Besides, I had already decided, in my independent mind, that this is what I wanted. So I asked, should I phone the store to obtain information on the status of the card? Perhaps the order had not been completed and the rewards card was not in the mail. Should I pick up the mat before they send it back?

The answer that came to mind was: *Just wait a few days, it will come.* So I waited another day, and still, no rewards card in the mail. I knew I had nearly two weeks leeway, but by my own way of looking at things, two weeks appeared to be cause for concern. Maybe I had heard wrong, I thought. Just in case, I decided to give Sears a call, at which time I was informed that there had been a delay in production of the rewards cards that month and to expect it by the end of the month, maybe. Well, I thought, good thing I called! I explained my situation to the agent on the phone, who advised me to pick up the item in question. She would leave a note in my file, then, when the card arrived, I was to phone Sears and ask that the amount of the card be applied to my account. And so I went out that lovely sunny afternoon and picked up my mat, now fully convinced that my hearing had simply been faulty.

Four days later, the rewards card arrived in the mail. Had I listened, I wouldn't have had to make that additional call to Sears, explaining again my situation, nor would I have had to make a trip to the post office to return said card with cover letter to Sears, yet again, explaining the situation, so they could apply the silly ten bucks to my account. All that senseless busyness, time I could instead have spent in quiet meditation. Although this event was really a non-event, it showed the extent to which I think I can decide what is best from my own, individual separated mind. If I had simply remained in the quiet and not crowded my mental real estate with all that senseless clutter, the matter would have been very simply resolved, with no extra effort on my part.

> To ask the Holy Spirit to decide for you is simply to accept your true inheritance. Does this mean that you cannot say anything without consulting Him? No, indeed! That would hardly be practical, and it is the practical with which this course is most concerned. If you have made it a habit to ask for help when and where you can, you can be confident that wisdom will be given you when you need it. (M-29.5:4–8)

Connecting with inner guidance is a simple practice which requires only that we be willing to quiet the mind, that we express our desire to receive help, and that we listen, again, with a quiet mind, knowing with certainty that help will be given. This helping presence can take many forms, but it always comes from an awakened mind. To ask for guidance is not only normal, it is welcome. The more awakened brothers and sisters there are in the world, the more examples of right-minded, non-judgmental, peaceful thinking there will be.

If it is helpful for facilitating communication, this guidance may appear as having a personality, perhaps even a name. Guidance that comes from the right mind will be free of judgment, it will take into consideration the best interests of all concerned, and it will lead to peaceful, kind and loving responses. The sincere seeker will find what he or she needs in the appropriate manner and at the right time. A peaceful, quiet mind will find guidance in a falling leaf, the smile of a passing stranger or even on a billboard on the side of the highway. Guidance has no boundaries, no set form, nor limitations of any kind.

Like the bent branch of the tree that is wrapped and supported, the bent mind of the child is gently straightened by the helping hand of guidance so that it can receive the flow of the life force that is its birthright. Awakening through healing then becomes a natural and inevitable occurrence. All the sleeping child needs is the desire to awaken, the humility to ask for help, and the willingness to listen quietly. In the asking has the help already been given.

> Peace is the bridge that everyone will cross, to leave this world behind. But peace begins within the world perceived as different, and leading from this fresh perception to the gate of Heaven and the way beyond. Peace is the answer to conflicting goals, to senseless journeys, frantic, vain pursuits, and meaningless endeavors. Now the way is easy, sloping gently toward the bridge where freedom lies within the peace of God. (W-pI.200.8)

Chapter 11

FORGIVENESS DEMYSTIFIED

> Forgiveness… is still, and quietly does nothing. It offends
> no aspect of reality, nor seeks to twist it to appearances it likes.
> It merely looks, and waits, and judges not. (W-pII.1.4:1–3)

A New Form of Forgiveness

*A*FTER A COUPLE OF years of study, we may believe ourselves to be well-versed in, and perhaps have become sincere
and dedicated practitioners of the Course's unique forgiveness process of looking, acknowledging ownership of what we have perceived as being a projection of what lies buried in our mind, and
then handing it over to the Holy Spirit for release and healing. In
its basic form, it is essentially a simple process, at least, simple in
the sense that it does not require endless analysis, senseless sacrifice, admitting one's guilt in public or punishment in any form. Its
power lies in our willingness to look beyond our misperceptions.

However, since our state of sleep is so profound and our experience of separateness from God is so total, one would imagine that
there might be more to this process than meets the forgiving eye,
otherwise we would awaken from our dream of separation after
the very first few forgiveness encounters. We might wonder if this
is really all there is to it, and if so, why is it that we must repeatedly
forgive the same persons or situations, over and over again. How
do we know that what we have looked at and released has actually

been released? How do we know that we have really, really looked and that the darkness is really, really gone?

In order to release the full power of this unique forgiveness practice, it is essential that we understand what we are up against: a thought system of separation hell-bent on keeping us in the clutches of its lies, no matter the cost. From the perspective of the ego, anything is fair game when it comes to its survival. Since we see ourselves as unique individuals with distinct physical, psychological and personality traits, that is, we see ourselves as being different from everyone else and are certainly not of the belief that we are all as one, the same, equally loved by God, it would be foolish to think that we are not under its very powerful spell. Given the completeness of our state of mindlessness, it is fair to assume that it might take a little time before we make our way through the dark layer of lies that keeps us from really looking. Not that in truth it need take any time at all, but because we fear the power of our mind to choose differently, which is, essentially, the same power that has chosen wrongly and holds us captive in a state that can only be illusory.

So it is that when we first begin to practise forgiveness, our attempts at looking at our dark beliefs about ourselves will be tentative at best; not for lack of willingness or sincerity, but rather for fear of uncovering the truth about our inherent sinlessness. As our trust in the process is strengthened, we are able to look more closely at what lies buried in our mind. The more we understand and accept that what God created can only be whole and is therefore incapable of sin, the easier it becomes to look at the darkness. The stronger our desire to experience wholeness, the less it matters what stands in its way, and the more certain are our steps on the journey home.

To catch ourselves judging our brothers is a very important step on the pathway of healing, one that should be appreciated, not only for its great healing potential, but also because it shows that we are able to apply what we have been learning. Since what we see outside is a reflection of what we secretly believe to be true about ourselves, it means that we still believe in our sinfulness, albeit a belief that dwells in a deeply buried recess of our mind, it is nonetheless a belief we hold about ourselves and, if healing is to occur, it must be looked at. This is the darkness that keeps away the light of truth, the darkness that obscures the goal of the journey. Furthermore, if we can be aware that we have judged our brother without judging ourselves for having done so, we are effectively in our right mind. Now that's cause for celebration!

Being that this belief in our inherent sinfulness is intolerable and cannot be repressed forever, now and again, a convenient scapegoat comes along, a person, thing or situation that is the perfect object for projection. Very often the ideal fall guy is among our special relationships: a parent, sibling, spouse, a former romantic or business partner, a boss, co-worker or friend. A scapegoat can also take the form of a political, economic or even spiritual ideology, a particular personality, character or even physical trait, anything that triggers in us even the slightest unease or loss of peace. Most likely, it is something on our list of pet peeves.

Many who are engaged on a spiritual path will firmly and sincerely declare that they have made peace with everyone and that there is no one in their life that fits the bill of scapegoat. We like to see ourselves as kind, thoughtful, peaceful, spiritual individuals. Keeping in mind that what is repressed must be projected, in addition to the fact that people who are holy, or whole, generally do not come into this world of duality, it is not a long shot to presume that everyone who is here, in a body, has some form of favourite punching bag somewhere.

If we are on a spiritual journey of sorts, the most likely scenario is that the ego, solely concerned with maintaining its existence, will have devised more clever ways of keeping from our awareness our dark secrets and our mechanisms of projection, thus leading us to be lulled into the false sense that we are on a peaceful, happy path of healing, if not outright already healed. If our intention is to awaken from the dream, this simply means that we will need to look a little closer; the belief in our sinfulness is there, along with the secret fear that we might uncover the truth about our inherent sinlessness.

Our secret sins cover the deeper fear that we might one day discover that they are just a trick, a distraction concocted by a confused mind for the purpose of keeping us from looking inwards. The truth remains always that we are sinless, as God created us. How could what God created *be* otherwise? The full realization of this fact places us a very short step away from accepting the Atonement for ourselves, spelling the imminent end of the ego. As might be expected, it is not in the ego's best interests for us to come anywhere near this realization so, if it can convince us that we have no enemies, not even one "button pusher," its safety is once again assured. Everyone has at least a couple of pet peeves. Simply recall the last time you said "This really bugs me," or "I hate it when people (fill in the blank)," or "Why can't they be more like (me, usually, as though that were a good thing)."

Knowing all of this places us in an excellent position to practise the unique and powerful forgiveness process taught in the Course. We simply acknowledge that this is what we have chosen to do, that is, we have projected onto our brother our deeply buried belief in our own sinfulness. All of which we almost automatically do because if we were to choose with the right mind, we would see the light of Christ in our brother, which would mean that, since what we see outside is a reflection of what is inside, we would also automatically know that we are sinless. Sin keeps the thought of separation spinning, and to perceive sin is essential to the existence of the thought system of the ego. Recognizing the sinlessness of our brother—thereby recognizing our own sinlessness—is the key to the Kingdom of Heaven.

As we know, the next step in our forgiveness healing process is to acknowledge that we no longer wish to see our brother sinful. We simply give it up to the Holy Spirit, the right-minded part of our mind that knows that sin does not exist. The Holy Spirit takes care of the healing part. This process of simply looking is at the heart of the Course's power and effectiveness; without looking, there can be no acknowledgment, without which we would not see the need to ask for release and without release, the darkness continues to hide the truth of our sinlessness. By looking honestly, without judgment, we are free to choose again, with the right mind.

But we're not done yet; not quite. As good forgiveness-practising Course students, it would be safe to surmise that the ego will attempt to devise even more clever ways of keeping us from the truth and, being the expert survivor that it is, this is likely what will happen. Imagine yourself going about your business, moving forward along your path, perhaps feeling peaceful—a dangerous state for those travelling with the ego—when you find yourself in an encounter with a suitable forgiveness partner, very often a family member. All of a sudden your precious peace is overshadowed by a cloud of darkness. This darkness may express itself as a thought of judgment, a feeling of defensiveness, or any emotion from mild annoyance to intense hatred, anger, or resentment—any sentiment that says that peace has been taken from me by what my brother has done. At which point, you begin your forgiveness process, during which you tell yourself that you must have been projecting and so you forgive your brother for what he has not done, you acknowledge that you no longer wish to harbour this grievance and you give the whole thing up to the Holy Spirit. You feel better and voila, you tell yourself, I'm moving forward and home is just another forgiveness opportunity away.

The Ego's Use of Forgiveness

You didn't think it was that easy, did you? Really? To think that being a student of *A Course in Miracles* would render someone immune to the ego's clever machinations would be naive. The ever-vigilant, non-discriminating ego will use whatever it can to keep us from the truth, especially our spiritual practice. Particularly vulnerable to the ego's slick survival schemes is whatever it is that we think is important, including our forgiveness practice. Many sincere students of the Course have made "forgiveness opportunities" something unique, something different from their ordinary everyday life activities. The moment anything stands out as being different from anything else in the world of form, it is very likely that the ego has had a role to play. There is no hierarchy of illusions!

In our application of forgiveness, if we have not seen that what we projected onto our brother is what we really believe to be true about ourselves, chances are that we were practising forgiveness with our good friend the ego. This would be the case if we had made even the slightest distinction between ourselves and our brother. We may have gone through the steps of forgiveness, but we know very well that it is our brother who committed the terrible thing that requires our forgiveness. "I'm not like that; I would never do such a thing," we reflect in silent smugness. "That's okay; she isn't a student of the Course; she doesn't know any better." We feel satisfied because we did our "forgiveness practice," not aware that the tiniest thought of judgment is a form of attack.

This is where honesty plays its important part. If we pay very close attention, we may find hints of our brother's behaviour in our own actions. In a twisted way—and the ego is twisted—we are quite thrilled and even relieved to witness such behaviour in our brother because we now have the ideal opportunity to point the finger outside ourselves. "He was mean, cruel and vicious, but I forgave him for what he hasn't really done. Thank goodness I would never do that." Now we are absolved of the sin we believe we harbour, at least for a little while.

The ego manages to infiltrate our thought process by making us and our brother different. To return home, we must know that we are all the same, as God created us, for we go home together, or not at all. With judgment, one brother is better than another. No one wants to admit that they harbour thoughts of murder, cruelty, viciousness, violence or any other form of unholy behaviour. Heck, most spiritual people believe themselves to be nice folks! The thought system of separation, to which we adhere if we see ourselves as distinct individuals, is built on a belief in a thought of murder. That's not a very nice place to start from. Just look at what passes for entertainment on television and in movies, where much unconscious darkness has a socially acceptable place for projection.

It is essential that we uncover the darkness so that we can bring it to the light and see it for the lie that it is. To hide it will simply delay our awakening and our return home. We are also told that we cannot pursue this journey alone; we need the non-judgmental help and support of Jesus, the Holy Spirit, or any other symbol of awakened wisdom. Only then can we safely walk through what we believe to be the darkness that lies lurking in our minds. The Course simply asks us to be aware that if we have seen cruelty, viciousness or any form of evil in our brother, it is because we have seen a reflection of what we believe lies inside us.

The normal reaction is to defend against it, find fault and especially, declare our innocence. However, the truth is, if we believed in our innocence, we would have seen our brother innocent, though clearly in pain and simply calling for love. The only thing to do is look at it and acknowledge that we have projected our thoughts onto our brother. The worst thing would be to deny it. The more we look at it, without judgement, the easier it becomes to release it. Nobody ever needs to know that we have had an unholy thought; there is no need to make it important or frightful or horrible. This is what resides at the root of everyone's belief about themselves, so it's not even a big deal. Everyone harbours the same beliefs. What else could be expected from a thought system that says: let's be what we are not: divided and broken and deserving of punishment.

Beware the Ego's Promises!

I have seen many Course students throw their hands up in frustration and despair as the circumstances of their lives failed to meet with their expectations. "But I'm a good *Course in Miracles* student!"

they cry out. "Shouldn't things get better? I'm a good, kind person. Why do these bad things keep happening to me? I've forgiven him; why can't he be nicer to me? Why won't she change?"

You may diligently practise forgiveness, you acknowledge that you are experiencing the consequences of your choice for the wrong mind, you give it up to the Holy Spirit and you feel at peace, momentarily, happy with yourself for having done as required. You are a good Course student. In all likelihood, you are undertaking this journey with your congenial companion, the ego. Take a moment to stand back and be vigilant for how the ego might be ready to use your good intentions in its favour. Yes, you practised forgiveness, as taught. You did a mighty fine job, given the circumstances. However, this forgiveness thing is a bit too threatening for the ego, so it will try to get the last word. From the back rafters of your mind, it suggests that since you have been a good Course student, then perhaps the Holy Spirit will smile down on you and provide you with a favourable outcome. You've been good; you should be rewarded. Furthermore, if things should not work out as expected, as often happens in this world, then the ego gets a double bonus. Once again, you are a victim of circumstances beyond your control, plus, it proves that you can't count on the Holy Spirit. Poor you! This is the kind of conniving bargaining thinking that lurks in the back of our still ego-allied minds.

In the beginning, it is understandable to expect that the practice of forgiveness will have a positive impact on our lives, leading to more favourable outcomes and opportunities, and at times, it does. In the Course, Jesus does promise a happier dream. However, the joy does not come from the fact that situations in our lives are being fixed; it comes from a shift in perception, which is a result of the awakening of the right mind. This shift in perception says that what is in and of the world does not matter; it declares that peace of mind is a more valuable choice. In this shift is the ego's thought system being undone; in this shift does joy arise, for the journey home is growing shorter.

A Helpful Shift of Perspective

When I first began to work with this new forgiveness practice, I found it somewhat confusing to declare that I forgave my brother because he had not really done anything, besides which, it was all my dream, there was no one really out there and the world was just an illusion. Though metaphysically correct, it seemed unrealistic and impractical when there was no doubt that a brother had gotten in my face. I could accept that what I was perceiving, especially when my peace had been disturbed, was a reflection of what I secretly believed to be true about myself since I had long been aware of the process of projection; but I found it difficult to see the whole thing as illusion when it was very real to me.

This line of thinking only began to make sense when I first took the time to rise above the battleground, from which vantage point it became clear that whatever my brother had done, in fact, what all my brothers and sisters appear to be doing at any given time, is occurring within the context of a dream, a make-believe playground in which endless scenarios are being re-enacted, over and over again. Whatever is being acted out in this playground is done while in a state of sleep, which, in effect, is a state of ignorance being that, while asleep, we have no recollection of who we really are as God's children.

While asleep and playing our games in our make-believe dream world, we are doing the best we can. Given that we are dreaming and have never left our home, we are never in any real danger, except the danger we imagine ourselves to be facing in a dream, and so there is really no basis for ever passing judgment on anyone, nor for taking seriously anything that goes on in the playground of our lives. When we are fearful, it is a reflection of our belief in our vulnerability; since God created us whole and invulnerable, this is a belief that only carries weight in a state of dreaming, in a condition of ignorance, an illusory state concocted by an insane, split mind which we know as the ego.

And so to be upset for what someone appears to be doing in a dream would be silly indeed. The only value in an experience in which we become upset, therefore, is that it reveals to us what we believe to be true about ourselves, for what we see outside, is a mirror of what we believe lies inside. With this awareness, we are now ready to give it up to the Holy Spirit so that the true healing can begin. Although an experience of conflict with a brother might have been disturbing to our peace, in whatever form it may have taken, great or small, it has served the very important function of bringing to light some of the darkness that lies within. Since it is only by bringing all of the darkness to the light of truth to be dispelled so we can eventually return home, catching ourselves judging a brother, recognizing that we are feeling victimized or in any way upset by what a brother appears to have done, is the best way to fast-track our journey home!

To say that there is not anyone really out there can be somewhat misleading, especially in the slippery hands of the ego. What we think we see, what is not really out there, is a misperceived version of our brother, as seen through the dark, distorted lens of the ego. What is out there, is God and His creations, including our brother who, despite his current state of ignorance, is truly whole and sinless. We did not make the person that is attacking us or pushing our buttons, but we did make up our mind to see that person through the ego's lens of judgment. We can instead choose to see our brother sinless, through the forgiving lens of the Holy Spirit. It is only in seeing our brother whole and sinless that we will know our own wholeness.

Chapter 12

THE CLASSROOM OF LIFE

My holy brother, think of this awhile: The world you see does nothing. It has no effects at all. It merely represents your thoughts. And it will change entirely as you elect to change your mind, and choose the joy of God as what you really want. Your Self is radiant in this holy joy, unchanged, unchanging and unchangeable, forever and forever. (W-pI.190.6:1–5)

A Compromise Approach

*M*OST PEOPLE SEEK OUT a spiritual path when they are experiencing difficulties in some aspect of their life. Perhaps they are tired of unsatisfactory relationships, or they are embroiled in a very conflicted and painful situation for which they have not found a suitable solution. They come to the Course because it holds, if not the promise of a miracle, then at the very least, a promise of peace, something that no one would deny that they deeply desire. They become students of the Course because they seek healing. On some level, perhaps not quite grasping the full meaning of its message, a part of them has seen that the Course offers a different way; it resonates with a deeply buried memory of the truth.

Pain, suffering or discomfort of any kind are powerful motivators for change. At least initially, most students begin this journey with the hope of fixing something in their lives: saving a troubled relationship, helping a child through a difficult adolescence, overcoming illness, finding light and hope in a joyless world, or even making the world a better place. In time, they discover that the Course says absolutely nothing about what to do in the world, how to fix damaged relationships, how to raise children, or even how to bring peace into the world, a radically different position from those with which we are familiar. There is no spirituality in the world today that does not, at least in some small way, involve itself in making the world a better place. However, with continued study, it becomes clear why this radical position is essential to this new teaching, in fact, without it there really would be no way out, there would be no true hope. To offer solutions for problems in the world would be to make the world real and the Course clearly states that the world we see is not real. If we had to solve the problems of the world before experiencing peace, we'd never make it. Instead, the Course leads us to the source of all problems, the only place where true change is possible: in our mind.

Many clients have come to me in desperation, wanting to know how to apply what the Course teaches in their lives so they could fix those circumstances that were clearly causing them profound distress. One client came after having learned that her husband of sixteen years had decided to call it quits. With their five-month old daughter on her lap, she expressed how she was struggling with the teachings of the Course, desperately trying to grasp at some semblance of order in a world that was clearly tumbling out of control. It would have been most unhelpful, and even unkind, to tell her not to make a big deal of it since it was all an illusion, while what she had known for most of her adult life was coming to an abrupt end. Nor would it have been any more helpful to remind her that divorce is painful because it is a symbol of the original divorce from God.

A few days later, another client sat across my desk, expressing how difficult it was to remain at peace and to apply what little she had learned as a beginner Course student while her partner was working up a lawsuit that was threatening to take away her home and most of her savings. Telling her to forgive her partner for what he had *not* done would not have been very helpful advice, nor would pointing out that she was valuing the valueless and since her true state in Heaven was one of abundance, she should stop worrying about such matters.

A highly successful businesswoman I met at a networking dinner confessed that she had tried to study the Course and do the lessons, but with three young children and a business to manage she had been unable to keep up. Sensing guilt and self-reproach, I told her simply that perhaps she should set it aside for awhile; she could always come back to it in a few years, when her life was more tranquil. Which seemed to me to be the most logical and sane thing to do; the purpose of the Course is to undo guilt, not add to it. At the end of the evening she approached me to say how deeply relieved she felt and how significant had been that little bit of advice.

So, how should students deal with life situations? The first thing I tell students is to not feel guilty for their inability to successfully practise and apply a spiritual teaching at a time when attention needs to be focused on mundane matters, especially a teaching that is designed to undo guilt. Nowhere in the Course does Jesus tell us to take an impossibly heroic stand while our life is going to hell in a handbasket. Sometimes it is best to temporarily separate the worldly life from the spiritual quest. Until a sufficient mastery of the metaphysics of the Course is attained, it is very difficult to apply this new thought system on a daily basis. This is a practice that is difficult enough to apply in the best of times, let alone in crisis situations.

This is why, at least for the first couple of years of study, it may be helpful to compartmentalize or, apply a compromise approach, as is suggested early in the text. However, to continue separating the theory from the practice as a long-term approach would lead to dissociation, a reflection of the profound resistance to the Course's message commonly experienced by students, delaying or altogether preventing progress on this journey. Since each person's life is unique, students must judge for themselves how quickly or how slowly they should proceed. One thing is certain, a spiritual practice should not overly increase stress, guilt or anxiety. If, and when, this occurs, then it is probably best to slow down or altogether take a break.

If you have been drawn to the Course or, if the Course has found you, it is because you have asked for help. Having asked for help is a very big first step; in fact, it is probably the single most important of steps to be taken on the journey to awakening.

Jesus, please help me.

There must be a better way!

Father, show me the truth.

This is the most honest—and most significant—prayer the sincere seeker can express because it recognizes that the previously chosen way of doing things, as a distinct, self-governing individual, separate from the Father has not worked. Though often coming from a place of deep despair, by virtue of the nature of the oneness of God, it is an absolute certainty that your prayer has been heard and answered. All that is required is nothing more than the faith to accept that this is true, and the willingness to become sufficiently quiet so that the answer can be heard.

Until you have learned to get in touch with the level of mind that is the true cause of what appears to be happening in the world, in most cases, it is probably best to go about your life as before. Nowhere in the Course are we asked to do things differently in the world. Do yourself a favour: if you have a legal issue, get a lawyer; if you have a medical concern, see a doctor; if you need therapy, find yourself a good non-Course-in-Miracles therapist; if you are ill, take appropriate medicine; if your roof is leaking, hire a roofer; if your job sucks, update your curriculum vitae and start looking for a better job. Avoid attempting to solve your crisis with the theory or the metaphysics of the Course; it is probably not going to work.

If you have a serious problem, and you are a serious Course student and are confused about what to do, ask yourself: How would I have handled this situation *before* I was a Course student? This will very likely be the best way to deal with the problem. Attempting to apply a thought system that does not acknowledge the reality of the world as we perceive it (or perhaps misperceive it, given our limited vision) to problems of a worldly order will only complicate and confuse matters. When in crisis mode, the mind is not quiet; a quiet mind is required to hear the guidance from the inner Voice that will lead to the solving of problems. A split and confused mind cannot fix anything on any level. A mind focused on quietly solving a problem in the world is more effective than a split and confused mind that is attempting to solve a problem from two completely different orders of reality. Regardless of the nature of the situation that requires attention, the most effective first step is to seek a quiet mind.

We Love Our Stories!

Everyone has a story to write, someone once said at a writers' group meeting many years ago. At the time, I wholly disagreed; who wanted to read a boring story, I remarked to myself. Not every-one had something interesting to say; some lives were simply dull. Naturally, my reaction stemmed from a mind deeply steeped in ego values: specialness, judgment, differences and hierarchies of interesting stories. We share our adventures with friends, partners, family members, neighbours and perfect strangers on the Internet, embellishing with just the right juicy details, not only to suit the style and mood of the story, but also to deliver the message we want others to believe. We might even bend or tweak the facts a little, just a tiny bit, to protect our broken self-images or perhaps to elicit a more sympathetic response from our rapt audience.

And as if our own stories weren't enough, we spend billions of dollars writing, filming and consuming endless variations of plot lines about villains and heroes, extraordinary adventures, the overcoming of adversity, love lost and love found. We make up silly games that we play with nameless strangers on the Internet, we attend plays, concerts and ballets with intense story lines. We watch "reality" television, read the latest bestseller, keep tabs on the breaking news of the day, and share hot gossip with our BFFs and our buddies at work. From the moment we awaken in the morning until we go to sleep at night, we encounter one story after another. And then when we go to sleep, we indulge in more stories, served up by our unconscious, unfulfilled desires.

Where would we be without our stories? What would life be like without our dramas, our mysteries, our plot lines and our complex interactions? Where would we be without our pain and our suffering, our adversities and our victories, our struggles and our triumphs, our sorrows and our joys? We say we want the peace of God, but in none of our stories is such a peace ever truly the desired outcome. Instead, our great stories deliver satisfaction in various forms of special love, revenge, success, triumph, justice, retribution, conquest, gain or victory. In none of our brave quests, our valiant efforts and our well-earned successes is eternal peace the intended goal, nor even the cherished reward. So how can we honestly say that peace is our goal when clearly, something else has always captured our attention? How can we say that we want to go home and simply be as God created us when we are constantly searching outward for fulfilment?

The ego is the ultimate storyteller and, being that we love our stories so much, it serves up the best plot lines in the entire universe, guaranteed to keep us riveted in our bodies, forever entranced and never wondering if there might be something else. To ensure that we maintain our belief in a world of separated selves that appear to reside in bodies that are clearly a most unworthy home for what God created, we need a riveting story, a script that is so tightly written that there is no room for doubt. And so it is that in our mythologies and our religions—our cherished testaments to the origins of our existence—we have a story of a Creator and His children. In these stories, the children behave badly; they commit what is referred to as sin. Fearing the punishment that must surely come their way, they run in search of a safe haven. In whichever way you dress it up, it is a story of sin, guilt and fear, and is the foundation of, not only our belief systems, but also our own personal stories. This is the stuff of which our dreams are made. The ego's story is the farthest thing from the truth and is designed to keep us from the truth. But, as long as we agree with it, as long as we desire our experience of separateness from perfect oneness, our perceptions will serve to prove that this is the truth by serving up situations that cause us to be fearful for our separated life. As long as we refuse to question our perceptions, they will remain as our only witness to the truth, and the world of separation and form will remain our collective fantasy.

Fortunately, Jesus tells us a completely different story, one in which he reminds us, unequivocally, that this world is not our true home and these bodies have nothing of the nature of our true being which is whole, spirit, as God created us, as thoughts in the Mind of God. If this be the truth, imagine the incredible amount of effort and strength of conviction required to maintain an illusion of a self that is anything but whole, a self that is encased in a body that must constantly struggle for its very survival, a self trapped in a body that is designed to maintain separation and destined to die. This cannot be what God wants for His beloved children, yet this is the belief we steadfastly maintain.

The biggest secret in the universe is that it is only our belief in this silly story that sustains its apparent reality—an apparent reality that will never be more than an illusion, a substitute for the truth. The truth is simple, Jesus reminds us: God is Love, He has never stopped loving us, nor have we ever left our true home in the Kingdom of Heaven. Yet, in our current separated condition, this sounds so very far removed from what we perceive and therefore believe to be true that it seems like little more than a lofty, made-up story. It is the very opposite that is true: this world of form is the fantasy, the made-up story; the Kingdom of Heaven is reality, the home we have never left.

Movie of the Week Starring (Insert your name here.)

Though we all come from the one Mind, appearing as split-off parts of a silly thought of separation projected out into what seems to be a world of billions of unique bodies and forms, as far as our experience in the world of separation is concerned, we perceive ourselves to be quite distinct from each other. Besides the fact that bodies are unique, what makes this belief in separation almost impossible to avoid is that each person's life appears to tell an equally unique story, a script that we treasure, nurture and cling to, no matter how tragic, sorrowful or dramatic it may be.

Although our dream lives appear to be unique, they are composed of the same raw materials: a belief in our inherent sinfulness over the seemingly successful separation from our Father, a preference for our independent, self-governing state, and a need to find something or someone outside ourselves who will validate this entire lie and go along with our stories. This insanity carries deeply buried beliefs in our murderous natures, guilt, fear, shame, self-hatred and a kill-or-be-killed attitude which must be projected externally. When we come into this world, this dark, fearful self-concept is forgotten as our attention turns to our survival as bodies. At home and in school, we are socialized to get along with others, and, motivated by a basic need to obtain what we need for our survival, we comply. While some learn to cope very well and successfully build a solid shield against this horrid memory, others remain close to their dark beliefs, living with constant thoughts of fear, shame and guilt.

Simply recall the last time someone you were just introduced to asked you to tell him a bit about yourself. How did you respond? You probably shared bits of information about your family background, perhaps revealing that you married your high-school sweetheart, how many children you have, your current occupation, where you were born and where you went to school, a favourite food, movie or sports team, a pet peeve and your astrological sign. You probably did not reply with: I am the Son/Daughter of God, whole and eternally loved by my Father. Though that would have been the truth, it would have been freaky, and perhaps an invitation to a bed at the local loony bin. Our identification with our dream role is so complete that it obliterates the truth of who we really are. Never do we stop to question this self-concept. Who am I?

No matter how well you dress it up, here we are, identified with a false self as a body fighting for our very survival in what amounts to little more than a made-up personal battleground that we call our life. How can we make our way from where we believe ourselves to be, that is, comfortably and profoundly asleep in a dream, to where we truly are, awake, with God, in the Kingdom of Heaven? While it is this dream that defines our exodus, it is also this very same dream that will lead us home. The quickest and most efficient way to make the journey home is to work with our unique script, our very own micro-battleground. As a highly individualized training program that not only respects, but also depends on the power of our mind to choose, the Course is not a bad choice for undertaking this journey.

Great stories sustain our attention because they make sense. Plot lines appear logical, characters behave in ways that are consistent, and appropriately satisfactory endings are delivered, as promised. In our individual life scripts, there seems to be a plausible cause for everything that appears to happen to us, and so, as in a well-written story, no one sees the need to question any further than necessary. Each person's script is unique and brilliantly designed to make sense to someone asleep in a dream, living in a world that is not real, identified with a physical body that interacts with other bodies.

We were born because our parents had sex, or a sperm and an egg were made to join; we have unique physical attributes that are caused by our genetics. We have certain character flaws and failings because of the way we were brought up, the bad neighbour-hood, over-crowded schools, poverty, lack of vitamin B, war, the economy—the list is endless. We have trust issues because we were cheated on by our former spouse. If we are ill, it's because of a virus, bad drinking water, or an inherited predisposition; if we are happy it's because we got what we wanted; if we are upset, it's because someone or something prevented us from getting what we wanted. There is an "it's because" for just about everything that happens in this world. When there is no apparent "reasonable" explanation, we say it's a mystery, or "God only knows," all of which leaves us helpless to make any real changes, since it's never really our fault anyways. And so we are born, we grow up, live our life and then we die. "That's life," we say stoically. Yet, we do not question our seeming helplessness, nor do we question what we call *life*.

My work as astrologer-numerologist has allowed me to witness first-hand the life scripts of thousands of individuals. In a way, it is like having a front row seat at the theatre. With my growing under-standing of *A Course in Miracles*, these scripts have taken on far greater meaning. Where I once firmly believed in the importance of, and also encouraged the development of, the uniqueness of each person's life script, I have since come to see how, on a deeper level, we are really not all that different. In fact, given the tremendous importance given to individuality in today's culture, many would be dismayed to discover the extent to which, deep down, each per-son's story is very much like everyone else's.

Many people experience recurring patterns in their lives. These plot lines can centre on personality traits, relationships, or on business or career choices. "It's my obsessive nature that makes me do these things over and over again." "I'm just an unlucky person!" "I keep attracting the same type of man." "I always get bad-tempered bosses." "I'm the one everyone always turns to when there's a crisis. It's the story of my life!" These repeating scenar-ios are the ones that most strongly define us as characters in the dramas of our dream lives, all the while reinforcing that there is an "I" who is experiencing something that appears to be very real. We spend tremendous amounts of time and money analyzing our lives, attempting to pinpoint the precise reasons for our pain and suffering—all of which is occurring in an illusionary state. Though in the world of dreams these stories seem to make sense, one must ask: to whom do they make sense? Beyond finding suitable causes for our dream-life dramas, what purpose does it serve to analyze them ad nauseam? The only helpful purpose for analyzing our scripts is so we can be familiar with the storyline we have adopted so we can then give it a different purpose.

Each person's life unfolds like a movie script, or the plot line of a great novel, and each script is conceived to convince us that there is a world, and that things happen in a logical, natural, normal way. In fact, we are all actors starring in a highly engrossing movie of our own choosing. We choose to play the role in the movie every minute of every day. Our co-stars have also chosen to play in our movie. We have all agreed to keep a particular story spinning, a story so riveting, that we will never stop to wonder if there is anything outside of this movie.

What we do not realize is that, at any given point, we can stop and say, I no longer wish to play this role in this story. The reason we do not pursue this option is that we believe we will cease to exist if our character is taken out of the movie. What else is there if there is no longer a "me" acting out with all these other people in my life? When we decide that we no longer want to star in our make-believe story, our co-stars will also have a choice to make. They can either find another co-star to replace us so that they can continue to act out their roles, or, they might stop and reconsider. "Hey, you stopped playing your role. You are no longer the same person you were when you were acting in our movie. I can't help but notice that now that you are no longer engaged in all of this drama, conflict, competition, struggle for survival, you seem more peaceful. I think I'd like to stop playing my role in this story too. Besides, as much as I have enjoyed being a star in my movie, it has not really brought me peace or joy. Maybe there is a better way after all. Thank you for pointing that out." In which case, your decision to relinquish your dream role will have helped a brother stop and wonder if there might be something outside the illusion of his dream.

Your Life Is Your Classroom

Jesus is a very practical teacher. Knowing that he couldn't get every-one into a monastery or seated at the feet of an enlightened master, he gave us a teaching that can be studied and applied within the context of our everyday circumstances. The best place to start on our journey home is where we believe ourselves to be, in our bodies, members of families with special relationships, with our own, personal stories. In order to begin the journey home, we must have our feet firmly planted here, now, ready and willing to examine our long-held beliefs about ourselves and about the world. Once firmly planted, we can take those first steps on the journey to awakening. Our life script becomes our classroom.

Not only is Jesus a practical teacher, he is also very knowledge-able in the best ways of teaching hyperactive, easily-distracted, materialistic, individualistic, self-governing, recalcitrant, non-holy seekers how to become holy, should they so desire. We asked for help, and though we may have been given a little more than we originally bargained for in *A Course in Miracles*, Jesus gave us a very efficient, time-saving and highly effective spirituality. In answer to the question, Are changes required in the life situation of God's teachers? Jesus tells us that changes are required in the *minds* of God's teachers. If he had asked us to make significant changes in our lives, we probably would not sign up for his lessons. Besides which, if he had asked us to change our lifestyles, our occupations, or anything else we do in the world, he would have been saying that what we do in the world matters. What the Course says is the opposite. It's never about what we do in the world; it's always about what is going on in our mind: we are either looking with the dark lens of judgment and separateness, or we are looking with the Vision of forgiveness and oneness.

Upon learning that the message of the Course is rather quite practical and must be applied in everyday circumstances if the student is to achieve its learning goal, many people react by attempting to alter their life's script. In extreme cases, some will quit their jobs, sell their belongings and travel to faraway places, or abandon their marriage partners and their families. The most likely explanation for these reactions is not a sudden onset of illumination, but rather a sudden attack of unconscious fear, the fear that almost inevitably arises as one begins to examine the darkness that lurks beneath the surface. Since the Course gears much of its healing practice toward relationships, once the ego gets a whiff of what you are doing, it will attempt to take you away from those precious special relationships you have spent a lifetime cultivating and nurturing. It is the practice of forgiveness, usually involving life-long special relationships, that is at the heart of this teaching. By removing as many learning opportunities as possible, the ego buys itself some time.

Your life is your classroom because you made of it your hiding place from the truth. In seeking to alter their lives, students fail to realize that, while our life scripts are uniquely designed to keep us in the illusion, at the same time, they remain the surest and fastest way out of the illusion when looked at with the healing Vision of the Holy Spirit. As long as you continue to cling to your separated individuality, your life script serves one of two purposes: the ego's, or the Holy Spirit's. Before making any changes, it is best to clearly identify which teacher has inspired the change. To attempt to change your life script without fully understanding its purpose, may lead to changes within the dream, but it may not get you home. It is only by giving your life a new purpose that change can occur.

Furthermore, if we were asked to change our lives, this would probably make things more complicated, and we already know that complexity is of the ego. Why make life more complicated than it already is? To use our life, with all of its familiar objects of projection makes the process much simpler. The only thing we are asked to do is to identify our choice of teacher. There are always only two ways of looking at any situation: from the perspective of the ego, whose purpose it is to keep us in the dark, or from the perspective of the Holy Spirit, whose purpose it is to bring us back into the light. The ego's version of anything is always a lie, and the less attention we give it, the less power it has over our ability to make choices. The Holy Spirit asks us to look, and ask, What is the truth here? By relinquishing the ego's purpose of separation and specialness, we are free to choose the Holy Spirit's purpose of wholeness and peace. But we must make the choice, and we must choose one, or the other, not both.

Will changes occur in your life once you have begun to work with the Course? Maybe, maybe not. However, after a time, you may decide to make some changes on your own. The common shift is towards a simpler, quieter lifestyle, one that is more conducive to the practice of listening for inner guidance and for maintaining a state of inner peace. However, none of the changes you make will come through coercion, none of these changes are required nor are they necessary for making progress with the Course. They simply reflect personal preferences, just as interests, tastes and preferences may change as we grow older.

Another error often made by spiritual seekers is to attempt to emulate the lives of spiritual teachers and masters. While there is much to be learned from those who walk before us, they are not the ones walking in our shoes; nor will we ever walk in their sandals. You cannot satisfy your hunger by watching someone else eat no more than you can go home by pressing the Home key on someone else's GPS. Take the bits and pieces that ring true with where you are on your journey at the time, and apply them to your life. If a teaching doesn't work for you, or if it ceases to work, leave it and ask to be guided to a new teaching. You have not failed; nor were the teachings wrong; they simply no longer served your purpose. The same with *A Course in Miracles*; seek those passages or those phrases that speak to the spirit in you and don't waste time debating their meaning with others. Spirit is wordless; seek to experience the truth that is beyond the words.

There are as many ways of returning home as there are dreamers believing they have left home. There cannot be only one way in a dream built on differences. The world we call our home is a place of multiplicity, and so the ways home must be many. This is your journey and you are proceeding at your own pace. Remember always that the only teaching you need is that you are as God created you, loved, forever whole and eternal, you have never been anything else, nor will you ever be anything else, and so the learning is really a simple remembering. Everything else is the result of you choosing to dawdle in the dream a little while longer. How long do you want to delay the inevitable return to sanity?

A Typical School Day

Your life is your classroom 24/7, which means that you are in school from the moment you wake up in the morning until the very next morning. If, at any time, you find that you are no longer at peace, then you can bet your lunch box that you got on the wrong school bus this morning. Take a look at the bus driver. If you are angry, upset, impatient, frustrated, feeling unfairly treated—*yet again*—or experiencing disquiet of any kind it is because you answered the ego's early morning invitation. And since there is no hierarchy of illusions, it doesn't matter if you are upset over a lost job opportunity, or for having tripped over a chair someone carelessly forgot to return to its rightful place, any form of upset serves the very special purpose of taking your peace away.

The ego says: Peace is not really a good state, in fact, it's rather boring. Let's find something more interesting, more exciting, something that will make my day worthwhile, something that will make me feel special, distinct, victimized, angry, even a little hurt is good as long as I feel something that validates my existence as a separate individual. It doesn't really matter to the ego what form it takes, it being rather indiscriminate in its choice of experiences. Its sole purpose is always to prove that you are right and someone else is wrong. You are innocent, while someone else is guilty. Which means that you're off the hook for another day. It's been a good day, the ego smiles, when you come home late at night, exhausted, discouraged and feeling that once again, the world was out to get you. How else should you be feeling?

At the first indication that you might have gotten on the wrong bus this morning, stop the bus and get off. One power that remains with us always is the power to choose our bus driver. Nothing in the entire universe can take that away from us. It's your classroom and you can choose to learn from it what you will. It's those in-your-face, day-to-day, ordinary, often very mundane situations that we encounter in our cleverly designed scripts that provide us with our best learning opportunities. Find a favourite quote from the Course or from any inspiring teaching that will get you back on track. There is really no need to further analyze how or why you are upset; you are upset because you chose the wrong teacher. Period. Now choose a different Teacher. End of problem. Peace will return. The next time a situation arises, you may catch yourself going for the ego's enticing invitation and say thanks, but no thanks. I prefer to choose peace instead. This is the practical part of the Course. This will take you forward on your journey home.

I am never upset for the reason I think.
I could see peace instead of this.
Forgive and this will disappear.

Chapter 13

BE THE ANSWER

The only meaningful contribution the healer can make is to present an example of one whose direction has been changed *for* him, and who no longer believes in nightmares of any kind. (T-9.V.7:4)

Don't Give Me No New Religion!

THROUGH MY WORK AND at business networking events, I've met thousands of people over the years and never once have I heard anyone ask for a new religion, and frankly, I don't think the world needs another religion. Fortunately, *A Course in Miracles* is not a religion, nor is it a cult or a church. It is a self-contained spiritual mind-training program designed in such a way that students can study, learn and practice independently of outside help and without anyone ever knowing what they are doing. With diligent practice, they will experience a greater sense of inner peace; as a consequence, friends, coworkers and family members may notice that they have grown kinder and perhaps even happier, and may enjoy just being in their presence. No one needs to know that you are practising forgiveness, or seeking the presence of God in each encounter with a brother or sister.

A mistake made by many new Course students who, excited about having found an extraordinary new spirituality and eager to share it with loved ones, is to attempt to convince their friends and family members that they too should join them on this path. During my first year of working with the Course, I lost my two best friends and many clients because of my misplaced, though sincere enthusiasm. Had I known the cost, I would have kept it to myself. Besides which, I really had no idea of what the Course was about, and so how was I to judge who this path was for? I've learned to trust that Jesus and the Holy Spirit will bring the answer to the ones who ask for a different way. That is their function; mine is to become an example of its message. Besides which, the Course came into the world at the dawn of the information age; it has already been translated in multiple languages. Chances are that those who have need of it will find it.

Like the works of many progressive and revolutionary artists, the Course is clearly ahead of its time. It will no doubt be several years, perhaps longer, before it is recognized for its effectiveness as a path to awakening. The reason for this is that its basic concepts are so far beyond what we, in our sleeping state, can understand, that very few people are able to actually recognize, let alone fully appreciate, the full extent of its message. Because it is so different from most of what we have been taught about the nature of reality and the origins of existence, it can take years of serious study before the student realizes what it is actually saying. By the same token, because it is so radically different from the teachings with which we are familiar, it holds true promise, for much of what has been taught to date has not led to a complete experience of peace.

As the first generation of Course students, literally suffering from spiritual starvation, many of us have plunged headfirst into its mind-bending teachings. Like a bunch of bungling spiritual pioneers, we have opened ourselves wholeheartedly to a spirituality that, for most of us, went far beyond our loftiest expectations. While some have stayed with its message, grappling with its powerful and uncompromising ego-undoing concepts, others have gone on to modify its message into something that is easier to digest. All of which is understandable in the early years, as we find our bearings and try to figure out what to do with a thought system that is designed to undo our age-old thought system of separation. Variations and adaptations of the message of the Course will come and go, but its core message will always remain unchanged: God has nothing to do with the world we see, the world, as we perceive it, is not our true reality; what we see in our state of ignorance is a picture of what we want to see, projected by a mind made mad by guilt. The truth is that we have never left our home in the Kingdom of Heaven, and God is all there is, right here, right now.

Most beginning students will look for those aspects of the Course's teachings that resonate with common knowledge, with something with which they can relate and understand. Many, if not most students, will ignore or gloss over the less ego-flattering statements, and some will reinterpret the teachings into concepts that resonate with what they want the truth to be. No matter the student's approach to this path, each person will derive what they need at the appropriate time.

For most people who have been touched by the desire to make the journey home, one of the first steps along the way is to find a suitable teacher and, what better teacher than one who is awake. In response to our collective cry for help, Jesus gave us *A Course in Miracles*, a twenty-first century, state-of-the-art spirituality, complete with detailed instructions, elaborate explanations, daily practice exercises and a road map. With diligent study, learning and practical application, it will take us home. Our choice of teacher and learning aids will reflect the goal we have set for ourselves.

Since most of us who are engaged in some form of spiritual quest have not found the simple words "God is" to be sufficiently convincing to bring us all the way home, in his eternal wisdom, Jesus, a brother who has it all figured out and is always ready and willing to help us, gave us lots of words in anticipation of our many questions, our deep fear and our resistance. For each question or objection that might arise, one is likely to find a suitable response somewhere on a page of the big blue book. This in no way implies that we are expected to read, understand or memorize every word. It means only that as long as we feel the need for words, as long as we cling to our questions and objections, our doubts and our resistance, our independent intelligence and our need to be right, we are likely to find, in its pages, words that will address our concerns. More than anything, what is really needed is an experience of the truth. Words cannot adequately describe this experience; it is simply something that is known. It is towards this experience that we are gently led. In the end, words are no longer necessary; love, our natural expression, simply is.

A Course in Miracles is a book. A big book. Actually, it is a very big book, but it remains, in fact, at least in print form, a block of dead tree sliced into micro-millimetre thin pages with a finite quantity of ink showing up in the form of words. It has a lot of words—probably somewhere in the vicinity of half a million words—no doubt more words than any spiritual seeker ever wants to read. And that very same book tells us that words are just symbols of symbols. Yet there it is, over 600 pages long, filled with symbols of symbols. But there is a reason why it contains so many words. Were it not for our lack of readiness to accept the truth, we would need only two words: God is.

The Course is not a holy book; nothing that is of this world is holy. In fact, the Course is part of the illusion. The only holy thing about the Course is its message of forgiveness. The rest is a teaching whose goal it is to lead us to a place where we no longer fear the only thing we really lack: the Love of God. Studying the Course will not get you home; practising what it teaches *will*. Without a clear understanding of its basic teachings and systematic application in daily life, *A Course in Miracles* will remain little more than a block of dead tree.

A Course in Miracles is simply a means to an end. Its goal is to make us aware of the nature of our split mind and eventually, bring about its healing. Before we can ever do that, we must learn to recognize the difference between our right- and our wrong-minded choices. The Course helps us to recognize which choice we are making, while reminding us that, at all times, there is an another choice at hand. There are many paths the student can take for this journey home, the Course being one among thousands. The journey home is about its ultimate destination, the full awareness that we have never left the Kingdom of Heaven. The journey home is therefore never about the journey itself.

Jesus does not ask us to study, memorize, and regurgitate the contents of the Course. He does not ask us to go out into the world, spread the Good Word, and convert everyone to this bold new spirituality. He does not even ask us to change our lives. What he says clearly is that he needs students who are willing to practise what it says, in their everyday lives, and be an example for the world of another way of looking. That's all he asks. And quite frankly, that is a rather all-consuming task in itself and should keep students busy for the rest of their lives.

> Teach not that I died in vain. Teach rather that I did not die by demonstrating that I live in you. (T-11.VI.7:3–4)

Show, Don't Tell

There is a whole lot of talking, and teaching and preaching going on in the world today, and thanks to the evolution of our communication technologies, all this chatter is available in just about every nook and cranny in the world. We teach about love and the healing power of forgiveness, we preach the virtues of kindness and above all, no matter our beliefs, we pray together for peace. Though we probably don't need a new religion, we do need examples of another way of looking at and responding to the day-to-day situations of the world. What the world needs is ordinary people, fully engaged in the business of their ordinary jobs but who have made a commitment to an extraordinarily different way of looking: they have forgotten to see another's interests as separate from their own. In so doing, they exemplify the message of oneness. The world needs people who inspire by their peacefulness, rather than by their worldly success, ambitions or even spiritual or metaphysical know-how. We need people who, by their absence of judgment, show that there are no differences, no matter who they are with, no matter what is going on. The world needs true forgiveness, for this is the closest we can come to an expression of God's Love.

Such kind, non-judgmental, peaceful individuals may attract more people to the message of *A Course in Miracles* because people will want the same thing. People will say to themselves: I want some of that! They might even say: "You always seem so peaceful, so kind. It feels good being around you. Were you always that way?" At which point, you might answer: "Well, no, in fact, I used to be very stressed out, even quite depressed. I was angry all the time. But then one day, I heard about this big blue book…"

This is what it means to teach by example. Live the message of wholeness, and it will spread to those who are ready to welcome it. Each person will then be led to the teaching, whether it be *A Course in Miracles*, or another teaching, that is appropriate for them. The message of the Course is already buried deeply inside every mind; what we need is to see how making a different choice, choosing with the Holy Spirit, will lead to a more peaceful experience. Love, kindness, forgiveness, peace—these qualities do not really need to be taught. We all know of the benefits of kind and loving acts. No one needs to preach this to us. No one needs to study and learn about love; this a peaceful soul knows. What the world needs is people who actually *live* the message.

There's a rule in fiction writing called "Show don't tell." In order to give the reader a firsthand experience of the story, the writer attempts to convey it in a way that shows what is happening through the actions of the characters, rather than by simply telling what happened by stating raw facts like one might hear in a newscast. An example might be as follows:

Telling

On his way back from the dentist, Bill gave up his seat on the bus to an old lady.

Showing

Bill slumped into the only free aisle seat on the bus; his jaw ached right down to his toes. Lord knows how he hated going to the dentist. Somehow, Doc Matheson always found a little spot of cavity in his teeth; bad genes, he had once remarked. This time though, he had taken out a whole tooth, along with a whole week's pay, and he wasn't quite sure which was worst. The bus lurched to a stop at a busy intersection, and more people climbed into the crowded bus. He hadn't noticed the woman standing next to his seat until she turned towards him. It only took a moment for him to catch the deep sorrow in her eyes and the weight of the world pressing down upon her shoulders. Somehow, the pain in his jaw no longer mattered. "Here," he said pulling himself out of his seat. "Please," he insisted. Seeing that the woman was about to protest, he said, "Take my seat. I'm getting off soon," which wasn't true, but he knew that she wouldn't take the seat otherwise. As he smiled and helped her into the seat, Bill lost any awareness of pain.

How much showing and how much telling is there in your practice of *A Course in Miracles*? Or, in your practice of any teaching? Are you a living example of the message of forgiveness? Of shared interests? Of non-judgment? The peaceful school bus driver who waits patiently at a blocked intersection, perhaps singing a happy tune instead of cussing at traffic, teaches a bus full of children that patience is a better choice; the peaceful factory worker who forgets to judge his colleagues when they arrive late at work teaches that we are all the same; the peaceful boss who listens with an open mind teaches acceptance.

Instead of teaching *about* love, *be* kind and loving with everyone you encounter, as well as towards yourself, too. Instead of preaching forgiveness, see your brother without judgment, including your grumpy mother-in-law. Instead of praying for peace, be the peace you desire, even with your wayward teen. It really doesn't matter what we do in the world in terms of job or occupation; but it does matter what we think. If we do things in the world for the purpose of acquiring more for ourselves, proving ourselves right, maintaining our separateness and nurturing our specialness, then we are supporting the world made by the ego. If, on the other hand, we do things in the world with the help of the Holy Spirit, with a forgiving attitude, with kindness and love, with shared interests at heart, we can all begin the journey home. In this way, instead of making the world any more real than it needs to be, we can use it to undo the thought system of the ego. Since we go home together, or not at all, each encounter is an opportunity to join. Each experience of joining takes us one step closer to the Kingdom of Heaven.

Be the Love, Right Here, Right Now

The following was taken from an article I wrote for my blog in response to the hoopla concerning the dawning of 2012. It was a simple call for making a different choice, for putting the power back into the hands of each and every living person. For those who might be seeking a practical way to become more self-aware and to remove some of the blocks to the expression of love, I thought it might be appropriate to insert it in this chapter.

Take a moment to examine your day so far. Did you treat each person you encountered with the highest degree of love, respect and dignity? The homeless man sitting on the curb, a daughter who just announced that she was dropping out of school, a cranky and impatient boss, your disinterested and increasingly distant spouse, the rude and inconsiderate drivers in morning traffic, a lazy and unproductive business partner, the waitress who served you the wrong coffee? Did any of your encounters today elicit judgmental, critical, angry, resentful, impatient, unloving thoughts? Did anything that happened to you today cause you to lose your peace? If so, look not towards 2012 (or any time in the future). There is work to be done, right here, right now.

Some seem to think that, given the current rapid growth and dissemination of spiritual teachings, an enlightened age must be just around the corner, and by all appearances, the potential for such exists. However, unless these teachings are actually internalized and consciously chosen and lived by their students, what we are experiencing will amount to little more than a whole lot of "spiritual noise." True spirituality is about spirit; enlightenment is of the mind.

From the perspective of non-dualistic philosophies such as Advaita Vedanta and *A Course in Miracles*, what we see happening in the world is what we believe to be true about ourselves, and since only perfect oneness is true, what we see that is not whole cannot be true. As such, perhaps it is time to take a closer look at our beliefs. The fact of the matter is that a shift in conscious experience can only occur with a shift in perception; in order for that to happen, one must have the desire to make this shift, and then one must choose to do whatever it takes to make this shift happen. Change has nothing to do with what is occurring in the world; the world as we perceive it is a reflection of what is occurring in our minds.

While more spiritual teachings are being made available around the world, we can at the same time expect to find more clever defences against them. It must be so, since the world is also used by our wrong-minded ego-identified selves as a mechanism for keeping us from looking inside, to where the truth of our oneness resides. The more busy we are with things in the world–even spiritual activities–the less likely are we to find the truth. War, disaster and suffering keep our attention focused outside and reinforce our belief that we are victims of forces—God, planetary transits, political ideologies, economics, calendars—beyond our control.

There are only two ways of looking at the world, and only one is true: we see either through the dark lens of the ego, or the light of Vision. There are either expressions of love or calls for love. When we perceive a situation in the world that is not an expression of love, the only truly spiritual response is love. To respond otherwise is to perpetuate the false belief that we can be what we are not. The only way to change the world is for each one of us to look inside and remove the blockages to the experience of love's presence.

We always have a choice in how we will interpret a situation, and repeated choices turn into habits. We either habitually see the love that is in all, or we stay stuck on the problems, misbehaviour, conflict, scarcity, suffering or pain. We have the power to create a new habit, right here, right now. We can learn to look at our brothers and sisters with kindness, forgiveness, non-judgment and acceptance, and we will see love, or a call for love. Either way, the right response will always simply be love. The choice is ours.

Do not wait for your brothers and sisters to adopt the same outlook; that is not important. The sooner you choose to see the truth, the sooner they will have a better example of another way of looking, but more importantly, the sooner they will have one less person with whom to engage in conflict. By taking yourself out of the ring, there can no longer be a fight. Choose peace instead and be the answer. Additionally, as more and more people awaken to the truth of who we are, humanity will be inspired to find more enlightened answers and solutions to the world's seeming challenges.

It is time to say "no" to the dream of separation and conflict and to wake up to the truth of who we really are. It is love that is at the heart of our being; it is our birthright. It is time to demand and expect an experience of this truth because it is what lies in wait inside our being, inside everyone's being. Right here; right now. This would represent a truly radical shift in perception! It is our choice; right here, right now. Peace will not happen to us; it simply waits for us to claim it. Are you ready to choose peace instead? Are you ready to experience love? And in so doing is the miracle allowed to occur.

Chapter 14

THY WILL BE DONE

Forget not once this journey is begun the end is certain. Doubt along the way will come and go and go to come again. Yet is the ending sure. No one can fail to do what God appointed him to do. When you forget, remember that you walk with Him and with His Word upon your heart. Who could despair when hope like this is his? Illusions of despair may seem to come, but learn how not to be deceived by them. Behind each one there is reality and there is God. Why would you wait for this and trade it for illusions, when His Love is but an instant farther on the road where all illusions end? The end *is* sure and guaranteed by God. Who stands before a lifeless image when a step away the Holy of the Holies opens up an ancient door that leads beyond the world? (C-ep.1)

*M*OST OF US HAVE been taught that God created the world and therefore He must be aware of what goes on here, an age-old belief which may warrant closer examination if we are to reach beyond the illusion. We also think of Him as a father in some form of body, a father who watches over and talks to his children. We are taught that if we pray to Him, He will hear our prayers. If our prayers are not answered, it is surely because He wants us to learn some lesson from our suffering, and so we should be grateful. He has a higher plan, a higher purpose for us, something we should accept with gratitude and humility.

But the god of this world—which is none other than the ego's version of god—is bi-polar: he is kind one day and wrathful the next; he has favourites, choosing some of his children over others; he loves us, then banishes us from our home in the kingdom of heaven for some sin committed long ago by someone we may or may not be related to. To top it off, he is cold, selfish and uncaring as he knowingly lets his children suffer and ultimately die. Besides lacking wholeness, he is decidedly not very nice. Clearly this is not, nor can it be, the true God. This is certainly not the kind of god I would want to go home to; in fact, I think I'd rather take my chances here, in the world. If the god with which we are familiar is not the real God, what then is God really like? How can I know Him? How can I return to my true home in the Kingdom of Heaven?

As was the common practice for good Catholics, when I was a child, every Sunday we would dress up and head out to one of the churches in our neighbourhood. Despite that these outings were mostly exercises in patient daydreaming, there were occasions when, given my innate childhood curiosity, I did wonder how it was possible for God to be present in all the different churches at the same time. And there were churches all around the world too; that was a lot of churches for one God to visit at the same time! And all those people praying to Him from all around the world, and in so many different languages, how could He possibly find the time to answer everyone's prayers? He must be really busy, I concluded, certainly too busy for me, not that I had anything of major importance to pray for as a youngster.

It was not until I hit my late teens, early twenties, at a time when the dark night of distance from God crept up on me, that I turned to God in prayer. But still, I did not sense His presence. I had been taught that He was there, somewhere, in some distant Heaven, yet, despite His seeming absence, I clung to the belief that He existed *somewhere*, only not for me. I concluded that He must be busy with far more important matters than my measly, insignificant misery.

It seems that my childhood church visits have recently been resurrected as Sunday afternoon lessons in how to be in the presence of God for, once again, on a Sunday afternoon, I was urged to go for a walk and explore what lies beyond the illusion. When not otherwise occupied with tasks that involved the application of intellect, I had begun the practice of quieting my mind, entering a meditative state, and listening for guidance. That day, having completed my newsletter, baked a double-batch of diabetic-friendly gingerbread cookies for our Thursday night *Course in Miracles* study group—okay, also to nibble on with my afternoon tea—and processed a couple of loads of laundry, I decided to settle down to meditate. There were no urgent tasks requiring my attention and my back needed a rest, and so it was the ideal time to turn to the presence of God.

Unlike most weekends, this time, I had been unable to write. It seemed that there was something I needed to learn before I could proceed any further. In a dream the previous night—or at least, I think it was in a dream—I had received instructions concerning my writing that had left me feeling a little rattled. In a very clear voice, Jesus let me know that sections of my writing required further editing. When I awoke I felt disturbed by the firmness of the request to edit my work. In fact, it stirred up some fear in my allegiance with my new teacher. Immediately the response came that if I was fearful it was because I was paying attention with the ego. If I had been paying attention with my right mind, there could be no fear, there would be only peace. Still feeling somewhat ruffled, and very much humbled, I switched to my right mind and went about my day as peacefully as I could, never forgetting the clarity of that guidance.

It was barely a couple of minutes after settling into my meditation, that I felt strongly urged to go for a walk. Okay I said, let's do it. It was getting cold and so I dressed up warmly. As I prepared to gather up some change and a shopping bag, I was once again urged to leave everything behind. I was to bring only my eyeglass case, perhaps my recorder, although I doubted I would need it, but no money. Only my key. I hesitated a bit, wondering if I had heard correctly. Why did it matter if I stopped at a store on my way to pick up something I needed? My daily walks were always purposeful and efficient and included a variety of errands and stops: the bank, the grocery store, the post office, and of course, daily exercise, and up until recently, listening to lectures on my MP3 player. But that day, as I stepped out of the house into the cool air, I had my glasses, my key and my gloves and that was it. Oh, and the recorder that would remain unused that day.

As I walked, I thought about the early lessons of the Workbook, wanting a better understanding of the meaninglessness of the world I see. What did that mean exactly? If the world I see is meaningless, what is it that is meaningful? *I have given all the things I see all the meaning that they have for me.* This means that I, as a perceiving self, independent from the Father, am seeing things as I would have them be. Everything I saw as I wound my way in a broad circle in my neighbourhood was attached to an idea I had about what it was—a sport utility vehicle that I might have preferred to my sedan, a redesigned front lawn with lots of space for visitor parking in the newly paved semi-arced driveway, a beautiful renovation on what was a very small bungalow, effectively doubling its living space—these were all meanings that I had attributed to everything that I saw.

Although I could very well appreciate the quiet beauty of the simple residential neighbourhood, I did not see God anywhere. Unlike my previous Sunday excursions, the more I walked and the more I noted items to which I attributed my own meaning, the more I felt myself moving in the opposite direction. There was no God in the way I was seeing things. There was no God in the meaning I had given these things. I began to feel lost and alone, trapped in the darkness of a world of form filled with meaningless thoughts about meaningless things. *My meaningless thoughts are showing me a meaningless world.*

It was a sunny day, but being early November, the sun was getting ready to drop below the horizon. I removed my sunglasses. There were no tears today. There was only the fear that I would never again feel that closeness to the presence of God. *A meaningless world engenders fear.* What I was seeing was not the truth. It was the illusion. It was a substitute for the truth. *God did not create a meaningless world.* What I was seeing was clearly meaningless. Where was God? What I was seeing was hiding the truth. God is right here, right now. The meaninglessness of the world is the illusion that hides the truth. I started to feel oppressed by the meaninglessness of my dark perceptions. There is no light in a meaningless world.

It was then that I decided that I would devote the rest of my life to seeking the true meaning of each experience. Father what is the truth here? Where is the Kingdom of Heaven? I wanted to remove the dark barriers of my limited vision so that I could see the light, so that I could experience the truth in everything and everyone. I had already turned the corner and was on my way home when I crossed paths with an older woman I frequently met on my daily walks. She was always accompanied by two or three toddlers from her home daycare, and her two dogs—stout poodle-like canines, okay, cute, clean and very well-behaved. Winter, like summer, I would see her with her beloved toddlers, carrying on conversations as though she were speaking with lifelong friends. No cell phone for this lady; only total devotion and attention to the young persons in her care. Since this was a Sunday, I assumed that the little girl she was chatting up must have been her grandchild. We exchanged friendly greetings and I complimented her on her lovely granddaughter, before we each went on our way.

It wasn't until the following morning, after having drafted this section, that it occurred to me that I had found the truth of what was meaningful when I had come across the lady with her granddaughter and her dogs. The truth had been right there. The meaningful had been right there. It was love. Everything else was meaningless. The only meaningful event of that walk had been the free expression of love between a grandmother and her granddaughter, and maybe her dogs. *Just kidding. I love dogs, really.* I thought about this as I stepped out into the chill morning air on my way to the bank. This time, I brought my wallet and a shopping bag; it was a Monday, and business needed to be tended to. But that didn't prevent me from looking for the presence of God while I went about my business. What was the true meaning behind everything that I saw? Houses? Cars? Trees? Fallen leaves?

When I reached the sidewalk in front of the bank, a car was turning into the parking lot. Contrary to what I may have done in the past, this time I did not accelerate my pace just a bit so I could get to a teller before the occupant of the car. That would have meant a me-or-him attitude, and I did not want to be in competition with my brother. I was seeking true meaning. It then occurred to me that, by relinquishing the thought of competition, I had given new meaning to an encounter with a brother, I had seen our interests as not separate. Instead, I had chosen love. Upon leaving the bank I saw two cars vying for the same space at the entrance of a mall across the street, one impatiently beeping his horn at the other, but I did not pass judgment on them. I could still love them, despite their choice to be impatient. I was looking for the truth. I was looking for God. I was seeking the meaningful.

Suddenly, it hit me. God is in my mind! God is in my mind when I do not judge or attack a brother. God is in my mind when I choose peace instead. God is in my mind when I see my brother's interests as not separate from my own. God is in my mind when I choose love, or when I see a call for love. God is in everything I see when I do not block true vision by substituting illusions for the love that is there. As I walked to the grocery store, I smiled, and I smiled some more. In fact, a few times I laughed. God is in my mind. That is the truth. He is not out there somewhere. He is here, now. God is in everything I see because God is in my mind. The first times I read Lesson 30, it never occurred to me that it could be taken literally. *God is in everything I see because God is in my mind.* God is in my mind when I choose to look with the eyes of vision.

Now, if you think the ego-identified self in me was thrilled with these new experiences, think again! It wasn't. In fact, it took less than an hour for me to accept the ego's option as the best alternative when it came to helping out a friend in need. Even though I had responded in a way that was kind, and helpful for the person concerned, it took only an instant for me to realize that I had so quickly and so easily pushed away love by finding a quick and practical solution for the situation at hand. The situation had not been the real problem; my inability to trust a brother had been the problem. I had acted out of fear. Gone was the meaningful; gone was the love; gone was the closeness to God.

I was unable to fall asleep that night, upset with myself for having screwed up, *yet again*. How could I so quickly and so easily have fallen into the ego's dark abyss! Now was a good time to have one of those conversations with Jesus. "I have a lot of doubt in my ability to do what I think you want me to do," I began, "besides which, I really think you didn't pick a good candidate for this job." A response wasn't long in coming.

"You are a good candidate because you have the willingness. Why make a big deal of it? You are already home, that is why you are a good candidate, and everybody would be a good candidate because everybody *is* home. What makes you a very good candidate is that you are willing to uncover your wholeness."

Still, I wasn't completely reassured. "Why is it so important for everybody to read about my screw-ups? Besides, I have a lot of doubts about my writing. I feel like taking all my books off the market and getting a job in a flower shop."

"Grab the recorder."

Fumbling in the dark, I managed to find the recorder and press the right buttons.

"You know why it's important that you write this. People don't get it. When they read stories of people who are already awake, those who seemed to awaken in an instant, they don't know how they got there. People need to know how to get there. You are telling them how you are getting there. And you will tell them how you got there. You are still afraid, holding onto the ego's lies about your unworthiness; that is your weak spot. And the ego exploits this very well. Remind yourself: How could a child of God not be worthy of God's Love? Remind yourself a hundred times, a thousand times, each time the ego tries to convince you of the opposite, remind yourself: What child is not worthy of God's Love?

"You will go back to the presence of God; you simply became afraid. It is a normal part of the process. It is not everyone who awakens in an instant. This is a course for people who did not awaken in an instant. If you did not have a course with a systematic practice you would never have the little experiences along the way that reinforce that you are making progress. You would not stay on the path. It would seem impossible. Keep moving forward. As you get closer to the end you will have more frequent and longer lasting periods of grace. This will make the journey rich and rewarding. Your strength will grow. There will be no more doubt. Your joy will be great. Greater than it was yesterday when you realized that God is in your mind. That is the truth.

"Have fun with your writing. If you think that I am too serious or too strict with you it is simply a lie. It is the ego's fear. The ego knows that I am serious about bringing you home. And *that* it fears. Stay with me. Keep moving forward. You will write this book. Tell it like it is. Tell it like you experienced it. It is important for students to learn how to make the journey. It is a journey. Although it does not have to be long or difficult or stressful.

"Though your confidence may falter and you may still have fear, your willingness is very strong and this is all you really need. You had asked to be shown the way home, and the way has been shown. I want to guide you along your journey. Let me be your guide. Simply allow yourself to feel the experiences along the way. Together we will write about them. Do not worry about the books. They will come in their own time."

Ignoring the part about "books" in the plural, having enough with this one on my plate, I told Jesus that I didn't feel good now that I was back in my familiar space, doing my own thing in this meaningless world. I missed the more meaningful presence of God.

"Now that you are back in your familiar, you realize that you are no longer feeling what you sensed when in God's presence. You are *feeling* it now. This is what I meant when I said you needed to allow yourself to feel. You see?"

I got it. That's what he had wanted me to experience. That's what Lisa had said. It was about the feeling. Not about intellectual understanding. He had wanted me to feel more. I got it. This was the experience. *Seek only the experience*, the Course tells us. In a reading from a year earlier, Lisa/J had pointed out that I had not wanted to come here, in a body, but had accepted to do so because of my love for J. It had been my purpose to acquire an understanding of the pain and the grief of the separation of body and soul, so I could share my journey of healing, share the return to spirit. I now understood what it meant to find the grace in my choice for coming here. My life, once again, had reached a whole new level of meaning, one that was truly meaningful. Having understood this, I began to feel better, and as hope and joy returned, more words of guidance came:

"From the ego's perspective, you are afraid that if you accept the Love of God and you go down that road you will cease to exist and yes, from the point of view of the ego, that is correct. The separated self will cease to exist. However, where you lack the confidence is in the fact that once the separated self ceases to exist, then your true Self begins to exist as your true being. This is where you lack confidence. This is where I am asking you to trust me, and this goes for you, who are reading these words, too. Simply call upon my help, and I will be with you. Trust that I will take you through this transition from seeming existence as a separated, false self to true Being as Self. We are here now. This is the part of the journey that you are ready to experience with me *now*. It is not something that you can do on your own because there is no longer an "on your own" that can function at this level."

"I guess this is what you meant by the slowly evolving training program, right?" I was thinking of the passage in the Manual for

Teachers, a humbling thought, if you ask the part of me that was eager to return home. But a happy thought if you ask my ego, for, the longer I dilly-dallied with the process, the more opportunity for pain, suffering and guilt, and hence, the longer the experience of seeming separation.

"Yes, but moving quite rapidly now, I must say."

"Thank you," I replied, grateful for my kind, encouraging, always supportive teacher. And although I could not see my teacher in too much detail, I knew that he was smiling, and so I smiled too, no doubt to the ego's profound chagrin.

"Thank you.

"I love you."

How could I remain upset with such patient, understanding and loving support at my side. We would go back and forth until there was no more fear and so the journey would reach its end, of that I was certain. I would relinquish incessant analysis and open myself fully to the trust that was needed to complete the journey. *Let Thy Will be done.* Feeling reassured, I set the recorder on the night table and drifted off to sleep.

The End of Words

The time for words has ended now. Though I lay down my pen, and you close the cover of this book, we will remain always joined, brothers, sisters on the journey home. We share a function in the world whereby we have the power to make a different choice and see the evidence of this new choice in the world around us. Together, with our Teacher, we rise above the battleground and relinquish the foolish, limiting misperceptions designed to hide the truth, and look now with true Vision. And if we momentarily lose our way, we dust ourselves off and keep moving forward.

Since we go home together or not at all, we remind ourselves now that each encounter becomes a Holy encounter as we choose the Holy Spirit as our Teacher, and, instead of seeing differences, we choose to join with our brothers and sisters. Each encounter becomes an opportunity to join, reflecting the oneness that is our true nature. And so the healing begins. We have much work to do now, and many brothers and sisters with whom to join. Each joining will be an opportunity to see the Divine in another, and to welcome it in ourselves. Each joining will reveal to us the truth of our wholeness as God created us. Each joining will allow us to know the love that is our natural inheritance.

Final Words from our Wise Older Brother

Be faithful to your path, but at the same time take only what you need to move forward on your journey. By the same token, be respectful of another's path. Do not attempt to understand every single thing in any teaching; there is no need. If you make the understanding of a teaching your goal, the teaching will fail its purpose. At one point, the teaching becomes obsolete and will need to be abandoned. This can be a distressing and even frightening moment. It is the point at which you must abandon self-governance of your journey. This requires faith. It is the goal of any good spiritual teaching. Each student's journey is unique; each student's experience is unique. Do not try to reproduce another seeker's final steps. Instead find the light inside that will lead you to your final steps.

Require more of yourselves now. You are not "*Course in Miracles* students," your brothers are not "non-Course students." See no differences between you and your brothers and sisters. You—all of you—are the Sons and Daughters of God, holy, sinless and loved, only momentarily imagining that you might be something else. Forget this world, forget your misperceptions. Seek only to know the truth. Join with your brothers and sisters and come with wholly empty hands unto your God.

I love you all.

Ego Flare-up Emergency Extinguishers

Although a simple "no" will suffice when it comes to addressing an ego flare-up, being unrelenting and increasingly clever in its efforts to attract and maintain our attention, it can be helpful to have a few spare emergency responses when we feel we have lost control. Here is a list of some of my favourite ego flare-up emergency extinguishers. Feel free to add your own to this list.

- Tell yourself that God loves you, no matter what, besides which, you haven't failed because you never left home in the first place. Chances are that the ego will have a few snarky come-backs, so, move on to the next item on this list.
- Ask: Father, what is the truth here? And if that doesn't work, move on down the list. ☺
- Forgive yourself. If you could have done it right the first time, you wouldn't be in this situation in the first place.
- Flip the switch on the ego, and move on.
- Don't analyze; you'll only be analyzing a decision made in a moment of insanity. Now, how sane is that?
- You are not the ego; the ego is no more than a bad habit.
- Remind yourself that you are the boss! The ego is a work of fiction, made up by a scared child, the part of you that is asleep.
- Be quiet and ask for help.
- Be quiet and listen for help.
- Be quiet and expect to receive help.
- Although this may be difficult at first, try peace, the ego's kryptonite. ☺
- Don't look back; just keep moving forward.
- Find a distraction, something fun to do, something that is more important than analyzing your screw-up.
- The ego analyzes; the Holy Spirit accepts.
- Remind yourself that your brother/sister is just like you, afraid of love.
- I am never upset for the reason I think.

- ❧ The ego always lies; don't even bother trying to reason with it.
- ❧ Don't ruminate, cogitate or try to understand why you messed up. You left your wholeness for a moment because you were afraid of love. Period.
- ❧ Your brother/sister is calling for love. If that doesn't motivate you to choose peace, see next point.
- ❧ We go home together, or not at all. Awakening is a two-person job.
- ❧ Choosing the miracle is a habit. It undoes the bad habit of choosing to believe the ego's lies.
- ❧ In case you missed it, just keep moving forward! ☺
- ❧ Go for a walk, listen to music, have a cookie or two or three.
- ❧ Call a friend or family member and talk about something that concerns *them*.
- ❧ Do not bring this up for analysis with your therapist, don't text it to your BFF. The point is to deflate it, and the only way to do that is to not give it any attention.
- ❧ The ego thrives and survives on the attention you give it.
- ❧ Remind yourself that your real job is to be the light for your brothers and sisters. Do it for them.
- ❧ Treat yourself, your brothers and sisters, every object, animate or inanimate, with dignity and respect, for all there is before you is God and His creation.
- ❧ If none of this works, enjoy the ego flare up, wallow in it, bask in it, but don't feel guilty about it. Then, try to recall what it feels like to be at peace. Peace probably feels much better than an ego flare-up. Next time, you'll choose differently.
- ❧ God loves you.
- ❧ Now move forward. ☺

BIBLIOGRAPHY AND RESOURCES

All references to *A Course in Miracles* are from the Combined Volume, Third Edition, 2007. Published by the Foundation for Inner Peace, P.O. Box 598, Mill Valley, CA 94942.

Edward, Pauline. *Leaving the Desert: Embracing the Simplicity of A Course in Miracles*. Montreal, Canada: Desert Lily Publications, 2010.

————. *Making Peace with God: The Journey of a Course in Miracles Student*. Montreal, Canada: Desert Lily Publications, 2009.

Lawrence, Brother. *The Practice of the Presence of God and the Spiritual Maxims*. Mineola, NY: Dover Publications, Inc., 2005.

Marchand, Alexander. *The Universe Is a Dream: The Secrets of Existence Revealed*. Tallahassee, FL: Inspired Arts Press, 2010.

Osborne, Arthur. *Ramana Maharshi and the Path of Self-Knowledge*. London, U.K.: Rider and Company, 1970.

Renard, Gary R. *The Disappearance of the Universe: Straight Talk about Illusions, Past Lives, Religion, Sex, Politics and the Miracles of Forgiveness*. Carlsbad, CA: Hay House, Inc., 2004.

Tuttle, Paul Norman. *Graduation: The End of Illusions*. The Northwest Foundation for *A Course in Miracles*, 1991

————. *You are the Answer: A Journey of Awakening*. The Northwest Foundation for *A Course in Miracles*, 1985

Wapnick, Ph.D., Kenneth. *Forgiveness and Jesus: The Meeting Place of A Course in Miracles and Christianity*. Temecula, CA: The Foundation for *A Course in Miracles*, 1994.

————. *The Message of A Course in Miracles, Volumes One and Two*. Temecula, CA: The Foundation for *A Course in Miracles*, 1997.

INTERNET RESOURCES

Please visit the author's website for links,
book reviews and additional resources.
www.PaulineEdward.com

Leaving the Desert
Embracing the Simplicity of *A Course in Miracles*
Pauline Edward
Desert Lily Publications, Montreal, Canada

After completing a first reading of *A Course in Miracles*, the most challenging read of her life, the author exclaimed, "Never again!" Yet, she knew that if she were to make real progress with her lifelong spiritual quest, she would need a thorough understanding of the Course's unique thought system. So, back to school she went—the school of life, that is. Though a seasoned seeker, never did she anticipate the dark nights she would encounter along the journey, nor the gift of grace that would pull her through. Readers will delight in the same profound spiritual insight, candour, humour and lively writing style as found in *Making Peace with God*.

"*Leaving the Desert: Embracing the Simplicity of A Course in Miracles*, is one of the most practical spiritual books ever written. I was struck by Pauline's ability to clearly and simply state the principles of the Course, from the beginning of her journey, through a genuine spiritual search, to her discovery of a new direction, to the understanding of miracles, and ultimately to the miracle of forgiveness in undoing the deviousness of the ego. I highly recommend this book to anyone who is on a spiritual path, and especially to those who want to get on the fast track."
—Gary Renard, Best-selling author of *The Disappearance of the Universe*

"I thoroughly enjoyed *Leaving the Desert* by Pauline Edward. It is an excellent description of the basic metaphysics and psychology of *A Course in Miracles* and its practical application in daily life, written in a clear conversational style."
—Jon Mundy, Ph.D., author of *Living A Course in Miracles*

"*In Leaving the Desert: Embracing the Simplicity of A Course in Miracles*, Pauline Edward shares her intimate quest both to fully comprehend the Course's fundamental principles despite the ego's formidable resistance and to apply its unique forgiveness in her daily life.

Leaving the Desert will inspire Course newbies and veterans alike with its profound, comprehensive understanding and specific examples fearlessly and generously drawn from the classroom of the author's life.
—Susan Dugan, author of *Extraordinary Ordinary Forgiveness*

"Written with humor and courageous self-disclosure, Pauline Edward's *Leaving the Desert* is a delight. Through sharing her own exploration—her commitment and her doubts—she addresses all the major topics covered in A Course in Miracles with precision and clarity. For new students as well as veterans of the Course, her overview of its purpose and methodology is excellent. Her adroit sprinkling of personal anecdotes enlivens and clarifies her path (and ours) and her honesty allows the book to be a comforting companion to those seeking to engage more artfully with this life-changing practice. You will read this book with a smile of recognition and gratitude.
—Carol Howe, author of *Never Forget To Laugh: Personal Recollections of Bill Thetford, Co-scribe of A COURSE IN MIRACLES*,

"Pauline Edward delivers the concepts of *A Course in Miracles* elegantly and uncompromisingly, and with an undeniably gifted style. This book is wonderful. It offers a deep and much-needed exploration of the core message of *A Course in Miracles*. It comes from profound guidance, and places the reader at the altar of Truth. *Leaving the Desert* is a must-read for any student of the Course, or any person seeking enlightenment, who would leave no stone unturned in an endeavour to return Home to our natural state of Love."
—Robyn Busfield, author of *Forgiveness is the Home of Miracles*

"Pauline's new book, *Leaving the Desert*, is itself a miracle. Pauline truly lives what she writes about; her writing is honest and from the heart. Her use of quotes is seamless and the whole reveals something that shines from deep within. This book reflects her process of returning home to Source; it will help you feel you are not alone in working with the Course. We do not walk alone, and Pauline clearly walks with Jesus and shows us that process. Kudos for Pauline and many thanks for this miracle look at the ego which helps to undo our own."
—Michael J. Miller, poet and ACIM stud*ent*

Making Peace with God
The Journey of a *Course in Miracles* Student
Pauline Edward
Desert Lily Publications, Montreal, Canada

It is said, "Seek and you will find." But what happens when your quest for the truth about life, God and the meaning of existence repeatedly fails to offer satisfactory answers? Determined to uncover the truth, you persist, and, lo and behold, you find. But what if the truth you discover challenges each and every one of your beliefs? This is the story of one woman's lifelong search for a fulfilling spirituality, one that answers the unanswerable, that is truly universal and all-inclusive and, above all, that is logical and practicable. *Making Peace with God* recounts a journey that begins with Roman Catholicism, explores various ancient and contemporary spiritualities and culminates with the extraordinary thought system of *A Course in Miracles*.

—Gary Renard, best-selling author of *The Disappearance of the Universe* highly recommends this wonderful book.

"A must read for *A Course in Miracles* students or anyone curious about its profound, mind-healing message.
—Susan Dugan, author of *Extraordinary Ordinary Forgiveness*

"*Making Peace with God* is the ultimate destination of all spiritual journeys… a story sure to save much time for the spiritual seeker."
—Alexander Marchand, author and artist of *The Universe Is a Dream: The Secrets of Existence Revealed*

"An inspiring and enjoyable book which will encourage others on their spiritual journey.
—Michael Dawson, author of *Healing the Cause*

"I recommend *Making Peace With God* to anyone who would like good company on the path!"
—Jennifer Hadley

"I simply could not put this book down. I highly recommend this book to any serious spiritual seeker."
—Jeanine M. Austin

The Power of Time
Understanding the Cycles of Your Life's Path
Pauline Edward

Llewellyn Worldwide, Ltd. Woodbury, MN

Don't wait around for life to just "happen." Develop a solid, successful life plan with guidance from astrologer-numerologist Pauline Edward. Whether your goals are personal or professional, *The Power of Time* will help you take advantage of the powerful natural cycles at work in your life. Simple calculations based on numerology reveal where you are in each nine-year cycle and what to expect from each year, month and day. With your life path clearly mapped out, it will be easy for you to pinpoint the best times to start a new job, focus on family, launch a business, take time to reflect, make a major purchase, complete a project, expand your horizons and more.

"I've used numerology for nearly 30 years. This tool is accurate, exciting, and helpful. *The Power of Time* will show you how."
—Christiane Northrup, MD, author of *Women's Bodies, Women's Wisdom* and *The Wisdom of Menopause*

"A top-notch reference, one that will excite and instruct anyone about the power of numbers in your life."
—*Dell Horoscope*

"This immensely readable book is a fascinating introduction to the subject of numerology. Best of all, *The Power of Time* takes the reader by the hand and shows her how to apply the concepts to her own life. I found the workbook sections especially helpful and could not put the book down until I had charted my own Life Path Number, Personal Year Number and 9-Year Epicycle. *The Power of Time* is a unique and insightful contribution to the many books available on setting goals and making short- and long-term career plans."
—CJ Carmichael, best-selling romance author

Astrological Crosses in Relationships
Understanding Cardinal, Fixed and Mutable Energies
Pauline Edward
Llewellyn Worldwide, Ltd. Woodbury, MN

For the first time ever, here is an astrology book that focuses on astrological crosses (the cardinal, fixed and mutable aspects of the signs of the zodiac) and their impact on people's lives, behaviour, actions and motivation. Crosses are so important to truly understanding a chart that you will wonder how you ever completed an astrological analysis without this essential component. *Astrological Crosses in Relationships* explores the strengths and challenges of each cross, using many real-life stories taken from the author's consulting practice. With this innovative guide, you can learn to identify crosses in everyday life experiences, mend star-crossed relationships and balance a lack or overemphasis of crosses in your birth chart.

"Pauline Edward's book helps us understand why people think and communicate the way they do, which in turn helps us to improve our relationships. That's no small feat! In-depth, well-written, and informative… A valuable asset to anyone interested in understanding human behaviour."
—Lucy MacDonald, MEd, author of *Learn to Be an Optimist*

"The best book yet about the nature of cardinal, fixed, and mutable. Her readable, insightful work can help both beginning and experienced astrologers gain much understanding about life's processes. Highly recommended."
—Michael Munkasey, PMAFA, NCGR-IV

"Absolutely excellent work on the cardinal, fixed and mutable qualities of the signs. Suitable for any level of astrologer, this goes into the subject at a deeper level than I've seen before. Thought-provoking and intelligently written."
—*The Wessex Astrologer*

About the Author

Pauline Edward is an astrologer-numerologist, speaker, *A Course in Miracles* teacher and Certified Professional Coach. She is the founder of A Time for Success, a consulting business specializing in Trends, Cycles and Lifestyle Planning, offering consultations and workshops for individuals and businesses worldwide. She is the recipient of a Chamber of Commerce Accolades Award for excellence in business practice.

With a background in the sciences and a fascination for all things mystical, Pauline's journey has been enriched by a wide range of experiences from research in international economics, technical writing in R & D and computer training, to studies in astrology, numerology, meditation, yoga, shamanism, the Bach Flower Remedies, herbology, healing and reiki. Her lifelong quest for truth and an understanding of the meaning of life eventually led her to *A Course in Miracles*, a study that has now become an integral part of her life. When not working with clients, she can be found indulging her passions for writing, gardening or hosting dinners with family and friends.

Pauline is available for consultations, coaching, speaking engagements and workshops. For information about services, upcoming events and publications, visit her website: www.paulineedward.com.

Lightning Source UK Ltd.
Milton Keynes UK
UKOW041459300412

191747UK00015B/219/P